I0144136

The Bible: From Darkness to The Light

Reading the Bible through in 26 Weeks

BIBLE TIMELINE	WEEKLY READING SCHEDULE

BIBLE TIMELINE

4000 BC—2300 BC
Creation to the Flood
2090 BC
Call of Abraham
1898 BC
Joseph sold Egypt
1446 BC
Ten Commandments at Mt. Sinai
1406 BC –1399 BC
Moses died. Joshua leads.
Conquest of Canaan
1350 BC—1051 BC
Twelve Judges rule
1051 BC—931 BC
United Kingdom
Saul—David—Solomon
931 BC
Kingdoms of Israel and Judah
760 BC
Jonah preached to Nineveh
722 BC
Israel conquered by Cyrus
739 BC—571 BC
Prophets Isaiah, Jeremiah, Ezekiel
515 BC
Cyrus allows Temple to be rebuilt
444 BC
Nehemiah rebuilds walls of Jerusalem
450 BC—430 BC
Malachi—Old Testament Closes
4 BC
Jesus is born
30 AD (or, 33 AD)
Jesus is Crucified, Resurrected and Ascends back to Heaven
30 AD—62 AD
The church of Christ began and grew from Jerusalem to the whole world.
70 AD
Romans destroyed Temple in Jerusalem
95 A D
John writes Book of Revelation, closing the books of the New Testament

WEEKLY READING SCHEDULE

WEEK 1:   Genesis 1—Genesis 35 : Matthew 1-10
WEEK 2:   Genesis 36-Exodus 20 : Matthew 11-20
WEEK 3:   Exodus 21—Leviticus 15 : Matthew 21—Mark 2
WEEK 4:   Leviticus 16 –Numbers 23 : Mark 3-12
WEEK 5:   Numbers 24-Deuteronomy 22 : Mark 13—Luke 6
WEEK 6:   Deuteronomy 23—Joshua 23 : Luke 7—16
WEEK 7:   Joshua 24—1 Samuel 30 : Luke 17 –John 2
WEEK 8:   1 Samuel 31—1 Kings 10 : John 3 –12
WEEK 9:   1 Kings 11—2 Kings 23 : John 13—Acts 1
WEEK 10: 2 Kings 24 –2 Chronicles 4 : Acts 2 —11
WEEK 11: 2 Chronicles 5 –Ezra 3 : Acts 12 –21
WEEK 12: Ezra 4—Job 5 : Acts 22 –Romans 3
WEEK 13: Job 6—Job 40 : Romans 4 –13
WEEK 14: Job 41—Psalm 33 : Romans 14—1 Corinthians 7
WEEK 15: Psalm 34—Psalm 68 : 1 Corinthians 8 –2 Corinthians 1
WEEK 16: Psalm 69—Psalm 103 : 2 Corinthians 2—11
WEEK 17: Psalm 104—Psalm 138 : 2 Corinthians 12– Ephesians 2
WEEK 18: Psalm 139—Proverbs 20 : Ephesians 3—Colossians 2
WEEK 19: Proverbs 21—Song of Solomon 5 : Colossians 3—2 Thessalonians 1
WEEK 20: Song of Solomon 6—Isaiah 30 : 2 Thessalonians 2—2 Timothy 2
WEEK 21: Isaiah 31—Isaiah 65 : 2 Timothy 3—Hebrews 4
WEEK 22: Isaiah 66—Ezekiel 25 : Hebrews 5—James 1
WEEK 23: Ezekiel 26—Daniel 10 : James 2—2 Peter 2
WEEK 24: Daniel 11—Amos 9 : 2 Peter 3—Revelation 1
WEEK 25: Obadiah 1—Zephaniah 3 : Revelation 2—11
WEEK 26: Haggai 1—Malachi 4 : Revelation 12—22

1st BIBLE READING MARATHON 2nd Ed

A 26-Week Through the Bible Reading Schedule

1st BIBLE READING MARATHON
A 26-WEEK BIBLE READING SCHEDULE

The Bible: From Darkness to The Light

Gresham R. Holton, *Ph.D.*
Contact: grholton@yahoo.com

The Bible Reading Marathon is designed as a tool to encourage Bible reading.

We believe the Bible is the inerrant, inspired Word of God.

We believe reading and studying the Bible builds faith in God.

We believe the life of a Christian is vibrant faith in action.

We believe faithful Christians make reading the Bible a daily habit.

For this cause, we also, since the day we heard this, don't cease praying and making requests for you, that you may be filled with the knowledge of his will in all spiritual wisdom and understanding, that you may walk worthily of the Lord, to please him in all respects, bearing fruit in every good work and increasing in the knowledge of God, strengthened with all power, according to the might of his glory, for all endurance and perseverance with joy, giving thanks to the Father, who made us fit to be partakers of the inheritance of the saints in light, who delivered us out of the power of darkness, and translated us into the Kingdom of the Son of his love, in whom we have our redemption, the forgiveness of our sins.

Colossians 1:9-13 (World English Bible)

Toni Webb, Copy Review Editor

© Growing Panes

Published by
GROWING PANES, INC.
3543 Raintree Drive
Valdosta, Georgia 31601

1ST BIBLE READING MARATHON

THE BIBLE: FROM DARKNESS TO THE LIGHT

The Bible Reading Marathon Series

This is a second edition of the 1st BIBLE READING MARATHON first published in 2013. Both the format and the contents have been revised. The first edition was a *chronological* reading of the Bible; whereas, this edition is a *traditional* straight-through-the-Bible schedule. The first edition is no longer in print.

The seven BIBLE READING MARATHONS available in the series:

♦1st Bible Reading Marathon²ⁿᵈ ᴱᵈ - **THE BIBLE: FROM DARKNESS TO THE LIGHT** (*Published 2019*)
    Theme: Reading the entire Old Testament and New Testament from beginning to end.

♦2nd Bible Reading Marathon - **THESE THINGS WE BELIEVE** (*Published 2014*)
    Theme: Topical readings on the major doctrines in the Bible.

♦3rd Bible Reading Marathon - **STANDING ON THE PROMISES OF GOD** (*Published 2015*)
    Theme: Readings on many of the Promises God has made in the Bible.

♦4th Bible Reading Marathon - **OUR GOD IS AN AWESOME GOD** (*Published 2016*)
    Theme: Readings on the Traits and Characteristics of our God.

♦5th Bible Reading Marathon - **ASK!. . .FOR THE OLD PATHS** (*Published 2017*)
    Theme: Readings on many of the Questions in the Bible.

♦6th Bible Reading Marathon - **IMAGES OF THE MASTER FROM JOHN** (*Published 2018*)
    Theme: Readings from all the writings of the Apostle John, including his Gospel, letters and Revelation.

♦7th Bible Reading Marathon - **GOD'S ETERNAL SCHEME OF REDEMPTION** (*Published 2019*)
    Theme: Chronological readings on God's plan of salvation from Genesis to Revelation.

A TIMELINE OF BIBLICAL HISTORY

Xxx-4000 BC	In the Beginning was the Word

CREATION TO THE FLOOD

4000+ BC	God creates Adam and Eve (Gen 1-2)
c2500	Cain kills Abel
c2400 BC	Noah and the Flood (Gen 6-7)

FLOOD TO PATRIARCHS

c2200 BC	Tower of Babel (Gen 11)
2165 BC	Birth of Abraham (Gen 11:26)
2090 BC	Covenant with Abraham (Gen 12)
c1900 BC	Job lives (Job)
1898 BC	Joseph sold into Egypt by his brothers
1876 BC	Jacob and family to Egypt (Gen 46)
1876-1446 BC	Israelites live in Egypt (Ex 12:40)

EXODUS TO THE KINGS

1446 BC	Ten Commands delivered (Ex 20)
1446-1406 BC	Wandering in the Wilderness
1406 BC	Moses Dies, Joshua leads (Dt 34; Jos 1)
1399 BC	Joshua/Israelites conquer Canaan
1350-1051 BC	Judges rule period (Judges, Ruth)
c1120 BC	Samuel Born (1 Sam 1)

UNITED KINGDOM TO DIVIDED KINGDOMS

1051 BC	Saul becomes King (I Sam 10)
1011 BC	David becomes King (2 Sam 2)
1004 BC	David wins Jerusalem from Jebusites
971 BC	Solomon becomes King (1 Kgs 1:39)
931 BC	Kingdom divided– Judah & Israel

KINGDOMS, PROPHETS TO CAPTIVITY

c760 BC	Jonah preaches at Nineveh (Jonah)
739-680 BC	Isaiah ministers to Judah (Isaiah)
722 BC	Assyria conquers Northern Kingdom
627-570 BC	Jeremiah ministers to Judah (Jeremiah)
605 BC	Babylon conquers Southern Kingdom

CAPTIVITY TO FREEDOM

c605 BC	Daniel and friends to Babylon
593-571 BC	Ezekiel prophesies in Babylon
605-539 BC	Jews in Babylonian captivity (2 Chr 36)
539 BC	Babylonian Empire falls to Persians
538 BC	Cyrus allows Jews to return home
536-515 BC	Re-building the Temple in Jerusalem
483-473 BC	Esther saves Jews in Persian Empire
458 BC	Ezra leads 2nd group back to Israel
444 BC	Nehemiah rebuilding Jerusalem walls
c450-430	Malachi written
37-c4 BC	Herod the Great and Birth of Jesus
c5 BC-30 AD	Birth and Life of Jesus, the Christ

26-29 AD	John the Baptist's ministry
26-30 AD	Jesus' earthly ministry
c30 – 33 AD	Jesus crucified and resurrected
	Pentecost, church of Christ begins

BEGINNING AND GROWTH OF THE CHURCH

32-62 AD	Gospel taken to the whole world
	Most of New Testament completed
32 AD	Martyrdom of Stephen
33 AD	Saul converted, apostle Paul
35 AD	Gospel of Matthew completed
36 AD	Cornelius, first non –Jew convert
44 AD	Herod beheads James

PREACHING OF PAUL AND NEW TESTAMENT LETTERS

44-46 AD	Paul's First Missionary Journey
46 AD	Book of James written
49 AD	Jerusalem Conference on circumcision
49-52 AD	Paul's Second Missionary Journey
	1 Thessalonians written from Corinth
53-58 AD	Paul's Third Missionary Journey
	Paul writes 2 Thessalonians
	Galatians written
	1 & 2 Corinthians written
	Romans written from Corinth
	1 Peter written from Rome

PERSECUTIONS AND GROWTH

59 AD	Paul imprisoned in Caesarea
	Philippians written from Caesarea
60 AD	Paul appears before Agrippa
61-62 AD	Paul imprisoned in Rome
	Titus, Philemon, Ephesians, Colossians
	Paul released from prison
62 AD	1 Timothy and Hebrews written
64-68 AD	Paul imprisoned again
64-67 AD	2 Peter, 2 Timothy and Acts written
68 AD	Paul Martyred at Rome
70 AD	Jerusalem, temple destroyed

END OF NEW TESTAMENT AGE

94-96 AD	Domitian continues persecutions
	Apostle John exiled to Patmos
	John, 1,2,3 John, Revelation written
c96 AD	John, the last living Apostle dies

I testify to everyone who hears the words of prophecy in this book: If anyone adds to them, God will add to him the plagues described in this book. And if anyone takes away from the words of this book of prophecy, God will take away his share in the tree of life and in the holy city, which are described in this book. *Revelation 22:18-19*

1ST BIBLE READING MARATHON - **The Bible: From Darkness to The Light**

MAKE BIBLE READING A *DAILY HABIT*!

God has always expected His people to read His Word. *"But regarding the resurrection of the dead, have you not read what was spoken to you by God: 'I AM THE GOD OF ABRAHAM, AND THE GOD OF ISAAC, AND THE GOD OF JACOB'? He is not the God of the dead but of the living* (Matthew 22:31-32 NKJV).

Readers will be blessed. *"All Scripture is given by inspiration of God, and is profitable for doctrine, for reproof, for correction, for instruction in righteousness, that the man of God may be complete, thoroughly equipped for every good work"* (2 Timothy 3:16-17 NKJV). In addition, reading the Bible will prepare Christians to do good work.

Like any good exercise program, reading your Bible will take a commitment of time and effort on your part. How much time will you devote to your readings? How involved will you become in really studying God's Word? Are you willing to pray that God will give you the wisdom to understand it? These are issues you must resolve to be a successful Marathon runner.

The Bible Reading Marathon program is designed to simplify your choices. The Greek Marathon is the base model for this plan. It was a run of 42.195 kilometers, or 26 miles. Unlike other races, the Marathon demands personal commitment and an ability to endure. More than 500 "Marathons" are run each year. Anyone can run in a "Marathon", regardless of your age or gender. The "winners" are all those who finish the race, rather than just a single person.

The Greek Marathon was probably in the mind of God when he had the writer of Hebrews pen these words: *"Therefore, since we are surrounded by such a great cloud of witnesses, let us throw off everything that hinders and the sin that so easily entangles. And let us run with perseverance the race marked out for us,"* (Hebrews 12:1 NIV).

———————————

Make it a HABIT. A habit is defined by the dictionary as *"an acquired behavior pattern regularly followed until it has become almost involuntary: the habit of looking both ways before crossing the street; or the habit of brushing your teeth every morning."*

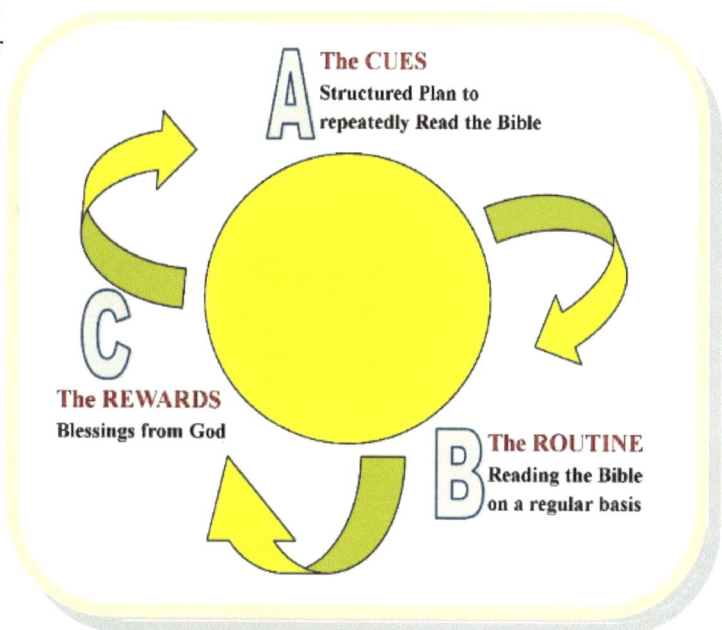

A The CUES
Structured Plan to repeatedly Read the Bible

B The ROUTINE
Reading the Bible on a regular basis

C The REWARDS
Blessings from God

Habit formation is the process by which a behavior, through regular repetition, becomes automatic or habitual. Strong habits become almost compulsory behaviors. The behavior is the actual habit that you are exhibiting and the reward, a positive feeling, therefore continues the "habit loop." (from Charles Duhigg, *The Power of Habit*).

2 Timothy 3:14-17

14But as for you, continue in the things you have learned and firmly believed, since you know from whom you have learned them. **15**From infancy you have known the Holy Scriptures, which are able to make you wise for salvation through faith in Christ Jesus. **16**All Scripture is God-breathed and is useful for instruction, for conviction, for correction, and for training in righteousness, **17**so that the man of God may be complete, fully equipped for every good work.

Make the Commitment!

The Bible Reading Marathon is designed for the young Bible reader as well as the more mature experienced student of God's Word. And, it includes all of us who are in between these two! Just select the "lane" you wish to run and make the commitment to read regularly.

♦ The **FAST TRACK** requires the most time and discipline. It is for those who are really serious about reading through the Bible. Runners who choose the **FAST TRACK** will read the Old Testament completely through (39 chapters) in twenty-six weeks by reading seven days per week.

♦ The **MIDDLE LANES** readings will take you through the entire New Testament (27 chapters) in twenty-six weeks by reading five days each week. Most runners will want to run in the **MIDDLE LANES**.

♦ The **INSIDE TRACK** is a compilation of many of our favorite passages based on research by the <*Biblehub.com*> on most requested scriptures on this website. The **INSIDE TRACK** also other Scriptures drawn from the readings in both the **FAST TRACK** and the **MIDDLE LANES**.

Yes! I want to join others in this spiritual exercise by entering the 1st BRM. I hereby promise that I will dedicate the time and the effort to finish the race. If I get behind, or temporarily drop out, I understand that all I have to do is just re-enter at the current reading. (I also understand that others may enter the race on any given Sunday after it has started.)

A weekly progress report may be given every Sunday morning, or, if you are out of town, call the church office and report that you are up-to-date on the readings. The posted percentage (%) scores will be the number reading based on the first weeks runners.

I hereby make the commitment to enter the 1st BRM race: _____

(Signed/Date:_____)

FAST TRACK
Old Testament Readings

WEEK 1
GENESIS 1-35   MATTHEW 1-10

MIDDLE LANES
New Testament Readings

INSIDE TRACK
Favorite Readings
Old & New Testaments

NOTES

SUNDAY
- [ ] Genesis 1
- [ ] Genesis 2
- [ ] Genesis 3
- [ ] Genesis 4
- [ ] Genesis 5

MONDAY
- [ ] Genesis 6
- [ ] Genesis 7
- [ ] Genesis 8
- [ ] Genesis 9
- [ ] Genesis 10

TUESDAY
- [ ] Genesis 11
- [ ] Genesis 12
- [ ] Genesis 13
- [ ] Genesis 14
- [ ] Genesis 15

WEDNESDAY
- [ ] Genesis 16
- [ ] Genesis 17
- [ ] Genesis 18
- [ ] Genesis 19
- [ ] Genesis 20

THURSDAY
- [ ] Genesis 21
- [ ] Genesis 22
- [ ] Genesis 23
- [ ] Genesis 24
- [ ] Genesis 25

FRIDAY
- [ ] Genesis 26
- [ ] Genesis 27
- [ ] Genesis 28
- [ ] Genesis 29
- [ ] Genesis 30

SATURDAY
- [ ] Genesis 31
- [ ] Genesis 32
- [ ] Genesis 33
- [ ] Genesis 34
- [ ] Genesis 35

MIDDLE LANES

MONDAY
- [ ] Matthew 1
- [ ] Matthew 2

TUESDAY
- [ ] Matthew 3
- [ ] Matthew 4

WEDNESDAY
- [ ] Matthew 5
- [ ] Matthew 6

THURSDAY
- [ ] Matthew 7
- [ ] Matthew 8

FRIDAY
- [ ] Matthew 9
- [ ] Matthew 10

INSIDE TRACK

MONDAY
- [ ] Isaiah 40:28
- [ ] Romans 8:28

TUESDAY
- [ ] Isaiah 9:6
- [ ] John 14:6

WEDNESDAY
- [ ] Lamentations 3:22,23
- [ ] Romans 8:38-39

THURSDAY
- [ ] Psalm 27:1
- [ ] 2 Peter 3:9

FRIDAY
- [ ] Jeremiah 29:11
- [ ] 2 Corinthians 4:18

Translations of the Bible into English runs into the hundreds (500-900) depending on if you include every version translated by one person. The Bible has been translated in part or in whole in over 1,500 different languages or dialects. The Bible is the most published book in the world.

Growing Panes

The Bible was written by about 40 men in about 1600 years--dating from 1500 B.C. to about A.D. 100. These men wrote as they were moved by the Holy Spirit (2 Peter 1:21). They wrote not in words of human wisdom but in words taught by the Holy Spirit (1 Corinthians 2:13).

There are 66 books in the Bible, 39 in the Old Testament and 27 in the New Testament. The Old Testament has 929 chapters and 23,214 verses. The New Testament has 260 chapters and 7,959 verses. The longest book In the Old Testament is Psalms. The shortest book is Obadiah. The longest book In the New Testament is Acts. The shortest is 3rd John. The word "God" occurs 4,379 times. The word "Lord" occurs 7,738 times. The prophet Isaiah is referenced 419 times in 23 New Testament books; Psalms 414 times in 23 books; Genesis 260 times in 21 books.

The Bible inspires us. It explains life and God to us. It answers some of our most important questions. It shows us how to live. It encourages us to rely on God for strength, direction, and to enjoy his love for us. The Bible also tells us how we can be saved from our sins and have eternal life. This, without doubt, is the number one reason for you to read the Bible.

1ST BIBLE READING MARATHON - **The Bible: From Darkness to The Light**

WEEK 2

FAST TRACK
Old Testament Readings

GENESIS 36-EXODUS 20

MATTHEW 11-20

FAST TRACK — Old Testament Readings

SUNDAY
- [ ] Genesis 36
- [ ] Genesis 37
- [ ] Genesis 38
- [ ] Genesis 39
- [ ] Genesis 40

MONDAY
- [ ] Genesis 41
- [ ] Genesis 42
- [ ] Genesis 43
- [ ] Genesis 44
- [ ] Genesis 45

TUESDAY
- [ ] Genesis 46
- [ ] Genesis 47
- [ ] Genesis 48
- [ ] Genesis 49
- [ ] Genesis 50

WEDNESDAY
- [ ] Exodus 1
- [ ] Exodus 2
- [ ] Exodus 3
- [ ] Exodus 4
- [ ] Exodus 5

THURSDAY
- [ ] Exodus 6
- [ ] Exodus 7
- [ ] Exodus 8
- [ ] Exodus 9
- [ ] Exodus 10

FRIDAY
- [ ] Exodus 11
- [ ] Exodus 12
- [ ] Exodus 13
- [ ] Exodus 14
- [ ] Exodus 15

SATURDAY
- [ ] Exodus 16
- [ ] Exodus 17
- [ ] Exodus 18
- [ ] Exodus 19
- [ ] Exodus 20

MIDDLE LANES — New Testament Readings

MONDAY
- [ ] Matthew 11
- [ ] Matthew 12

TUESDAY
- [ ] Matthew 13
- [ ] Matthew 14

WEDNESDAY
- [ ] Matthew 15
- [ ] Matthew 16

THURSDAY
- [ ] Matthew 17
- [ ] Matthew 18

FRIDAY
- [ ] Matthew 19
- [ ] Matthew 20

INSIDE TRACK — Favorite Readings Old & New Testaments

MONDAY
- [ ] Joshua 1:9
- [ ] Matthew 1:21

TUESDAY
- [ ] Proverbs 3:5-6
- [ ] Matthew 4:19

WEDNESDAY
- [ ] Psalm 16:8
- [ ] Matthew 5:11-12

THURSDAY
- [ ] Psalm 23
- [ ] Matthew 5:16

FRIDAY
- [ ] Psalm 31:24
- [ ] Matthew 6:9-13

NOTES

Growing Panes

In April of 1539, the first edition of the Great Bible appeared, also known as the "Cromwell Bible," the "Cranmer Bible, and the "Chained Bible." Thomas Cromwell had charged the clergy that they make a copy to be set up in every church. He commanded that "*one book of the Bible of the largest volume in English, and the same set up in some convenient place within the said church that ye have care of, whereas your parishioners may most commodiously resort to the same and read it.*" In addition, a reader was appointed so that everyone, including the illiterate, could learn the Word of God as they desired.

With this action, the large beautiful Great Bible, funded by King Henry VIII, became the first Bible authorized by the government for public use.

It became known as the "chained Bible" because it was chained to the pulpits. But, the Great Bible helped rekindle the desire to own a personal copy of the Word of God, and sparked a flame in the hearts of those who would later translate the Geneva Bible, the Bishop's Bible, and the King James Version.

The goal was to make the Bible available for the public to read, but the result of chaining it to the pulpit conveyed the message that only the clergy could authoritatively interpret the Bible.

1ST BIBLE READING MARATHON - The Bible: From Darkness to The Light

FAST TRACK

Old Testament Readings

MIDDLE LANES   **INSIDE TRACK**   **NOTES**

New Testament Reading   Favorite Readings Old & New Testaments

SUNDAY
- [ ] Exodus 21
- [ ] Exodus 22
- [ ] Exodus 23
- [ ] Exodus 24
- [ ] Exodus 25

MONDAY
- [ ] Exodus 26
- [ ] Exodus 27
- [ ] Exodus 28
- [ ] Exodus 29
- [ ] Exodus 30

TUESDAY
- [ ] Exodus 31
- [ ] Exodus 32
- [ ] Exodus 33
- [ ] Exodus 34
- [ ] Exodus 35

WEDNESDAY
- [ ] Exodus 36
- [ ] Exodus 37
- [ ] Exodus 38
- [ ] Exodus 39
- [ ] Exodus 40

THURSDAY
- [ ] Leviticus 1
- [ ] Leviticus 2
- [ ] Leviticus 3
- [ ] Leviticus 4
- [ ] Leviticus 5

FRIDAY
- [ ] Leviticus 6
- [ ] Leviticus 7
- [ ] Leviticus 8
- [ ] Leviticus 9
- [ ] Leviticus 10

SATURDAY
- [ ] Leviticus 11
- [ ] Leviticus 12
- [ ] Leviticus 13
- [ ] Leviticus 14
- [ ] Leviticus 15

MONDAY
- [ ] Matthew 21
- [ ] Matthew 22

TUESDAY
- [ ] Matthew 23
- [ ] Matthew 24

WEDNESDAY
- [ ] Matthew 25
- [ ] Matthew 26

THURSDAY
- [ ] Matthew 27
- [ ] Matthew 28

FRIDAY
- [ ] Mark 1
- [ ] Mark 2

MONDAY
- [ ] Psalm 55:22
- [ ] John 10:27-29

TUESDAY
- [ ] Psalm 119:114-115
- [ ] John 11:23-26

WEDNESDAY
- [ ] Psalm 120:1
- [ ] 1 Corinthians 15:20-23

THURSDAY
- [ ] Isaiah 26:3
- [ ] 1 Corinthians 15:54-57

FRIDAY
- [ ] Isaiah 40:31
- [ ] 2 Corinthians 5:6-8

Growing Panes

The Bible was not a book the general public was familiar with during the dark ages. Most individuals or families could not own one. And, as noted earlier the public Bibles were chained to the pulpit. Some copies of manuscripts of Bibles were in monasteries. The Latin Vulgate was the "official" Bible of the church. Bibles were owned by kings and the socially elite. But the Bible was not generally owned by the public at large.

Martin Luther and John Wycliffe were among the early churchmen to relieve this problem by translating it for public distribution. Luther started comparing the Vulgate with the original Greek New Testament. He discovered numerous mistakes in translation. That led Luther to another realization: if things really going to change, it would not come just by debating theology with other learned souls. The Bible needed to be made available in the vernacular (in this case German) and needed to be widely available. Like Luther's efforts, Wycliffe's work was not authorized by any ecclesiastical or royal authority, but it became enormously popular.

William Tyndale lived from 1494–1536 and was martyred for translating the Bible into English. Tyndale, like Luther, translated directly from the Hebrew and the Greek. He actually only finished the New Testament, completing about half of his Old Testament translation before his death. His was the first mass-produced Bible in English.

1ST BIBLE READING MARATHON - **The Bible: From Darkness to The Light**

WEEK 4

LEVITICUS 15-NUMBERS 23 · MARK 3-12

FAST TRACK

Old Testament Readings

SUNDAY
- [ ] Leviticus 16
- [ ] Leviticus 17
- [ ] Leviticus 18
- [ ] Leviticus 19
- [ ] Leviticus 20

MONDAY
- [ ] Leviticus 21
- [ ] Leviticus 22
- [ ] Leviticus 23
- [ ] Leviticus 24
- [ ] Leviticus 25

TUESDAY
- [ ] Leviticus 26
- [ ] Leviticus 27
- [ ] Numbers 1
- [ ] Numbers 2
- [ ] Numbers 3

WEDNESDAY
- [ ] Numbers 4
- [ ] Numbers 5
- [ ] Numbers 6
- [ ] Numbers 7
- [ ] Numbers 8

THURSDAY
- [ ] Numbers 9
- [ ] Numbers 10
- [ ] Numbers 11
- [ ] Numbers 12
- [ ] Numbers 13

FRIDAY
- [ ] Numbers 14
- [ ] Numbers 15
- [ ] Numbers 16
- [ ] Numbers 17
- [ ] Numbers 18

SATURDAY
- [ ] Numbers 19
- [ ] Numbers 20
- [ ] Numbers 21
- [ ] Numbers 22
- [ ] Numbers 23

MIDDLE LANES

New Testament Readings

MONDAY
- [ ] Mark 3
- [ ] Mark 4

TUESDAY
- [ ] Mark 5
- [ ] Mark 6

WEDNESDAY
- [ ] Mark 7
- [ ] Mark 8

THURSDAY
- [ ] Mark 9
- [ ] Mark 10

FRIDAY
- [ ] Mark 11
- [ ] Mark 12

INSIDE TRACK

Favorite Readings Old & New Testaments

MONDAY
- [ ] Psalm 39:4
- [ ] 1 Thessalonians 5:9-11

TUESDAY
- [ ] Psalm 116:15
- [ ] Revelation 2:10

WEDNESDAY
- [ ] Ecclesiastes 3:1-4
- [ ] Matthew 11:28

THURSDAY
- [ ] Isaiah 53:4-5
- [ ] Revelation 14:13

FRIDAY
- [ ] Hosea 13:14
- [ ] Romans 15:4

NOTES

Growing Panes

Over the centuries, Satan the devil has incited and inflamed every imaginable plot to extinguish the light of God's truth. The Bible, and how it has survived, is the miracle of the ages.

Soon after the beginning of the New Testament Church, "a great persecution arose against the church which was at Jerusalem; and they were all scattered" (Acts 8:1). However, this worked for good to spread God's Word. "Therefore, those who were scattered went everywhere preaching the word" (Acts 8:4).

For hundreds of years leading up to the late Middle Ages, religious leaders frequently confiscated and burned Bibles. People were often put to death merely for having a portion of the Bible in their possession.

The Scriptures survived not only because of God's divine protection, but also because of the faith and zeal of His people. They knew they had "*the pearl of great price*" and were willing to risk their lives to protect, preserve and propagate it (Matthew 13:46). Their zeal to make copies and distribute them made it difficult for enemies to find and destroy all the copies.

"The grass withers, the flower fades, but the word of our God stands forever" (Isaiah 40:8).

WEEK 5

FAST TRACK
Old Testament Readings

SUNDAY
- [ ] Numbers 24
- [ ] Numbers 25
- [ ] Numbers 26
- [ ] Numbers 27
- [ ] Numbers 28

MONDAY
- [ ] Numbers 29
- [ ] Numbers 30
- [ ] Numbers 31
- [ ] Numbers 32
- [ ] Numbers 33

TUESDAY
- [ ] Numbers 34
- [ ] Numbers 35
- [ ] Numbers 36
- [ ] Deuteronomy 1
- [ ] Deuteronomy 2

WEDNESDAY
- [ ] Deuteronomy 3
- [ ] Deuteronomy 4
- [ ] Deuteronomy 5
- [ ] Deuteronomy 6
- [ ] Deuteronomy 7

THURSDAY
- [ ] Deuteronomy 8
- [ ] Deuteronomy 9
- [ ] Deuteronomy 10
- [ ] Deuteronomy 11
- [ ] Deuteronomy 12

FRIDAY
- [ ] Deuteronomy 13
- [ ] Deuteronomy 14
- [ ] Deuteronomy 15
- [ ] Deuteronomy 16
- [ ] Deuteronomy 17

SATURDAY
- [ ] Deuteronomy 18
- [ ] Deuteronomy 19
- [ ] Deuteronomy 20
- [ ] Deuteronomy 21
- [ ] Deuteronomy 22

MIDDLE LANES
New Testament Readings

MONDAY
- [ ] Mark 13
- [ ] Mark 14

TUESDAY
- [ ] Mark 15
- [ ] Mark 16

WEDNESDAY
- [ ] Luke 1
- [ ] Luke 2

THURSDAY
- [ ] Luke 3
- [ ] Luke 4

FRIDAY
- [ ] Luke 5
- [ ] Luke 6

INSIDE TRACK
Favorite Readings Old & New Testaments

MONDAY
- [ ] Psalm 18:28
- [ ] 2 Corinthians 12:9

TUESDAY
- [ ] Psalm 27:4-5
- [ ] Philippians 4: 12-13

WEDNESDAY
- [ ] Psalm 46:1-3
- [ ] 1 Peter 5: 10

THURSDAY
- [ ] Nehemiah 8:10
- [ ] 2 Thessalonians 3:3

FRIDAY
- [ ] Isaiah 41:10
- [ ] Hebrews 4:16

NOTES

Growing Panes

God's intention and desire to bless humanity is a central focus of the Bible. Two distinct ideas are present in the many passages. First, a blessing was a public declaration of a favored status with God. Second, the blessing endowed power for prosperity and success. In all cases, the blessing served as a guide and motivation to pursue a course of life within the blessing. A general blessing is bestowed on the righteous. Those who are obedient to God's commands are blessed with affluence and victory (Deuteronomy 28:1-14).

In a general sense, the terms for blessing in the New Testament are used to designate that one is favored by God. Included among these are Jesus (Mark 11:9-10); children (Mark 10:13-16); Mary (Luke 1:42; Luke 1:48); the disciples (Luke 24:50); those who "have not seen and yet have believed" (John 20:29); and those who endure trials (James 1:12 ; 5:11).

The most recognizable references to blessing come from the teachings of Jesus. He declares that in spite of difficulties at the present time, the promises of God's salvation brings a state of happiness and recognized favor with God (Matthew 5:3-10 ; Luke 6:20-22). The culmination of the Scriptures proclaims the end of the curse (Revelation 22:3) and the eternal blessedness of the people of God (Revelation 20:6 ; 22:7).

1ST BIBLE READING MARATHON   - **The Bible: From Darkness to The Light**

FAST TRACK
Old Testament Readings

DEUTERONOMY 23-JOSHUA 23 WEEK 6   LUKE 7-16

MIDDLE LANES
New Testament Readings

INSIDE TRACK
Favorite Readings Old & New Testaments

NOTES

SUNDAY
- [ ] Deuteronomy 23
- [ ] Deuteronomy 24
- [ ] Deuteronomy 25
- [ ] Deuteronomy 26
- [ ] Deuteronomy 27

MONDAY
- [ ] Deuteronomy 28
- [ ] Deuteronomy 29
- [ ] Deuteronomy 30
- [ ] Deuteronomy 31
- [ ] Deuteronomy 32

TUESDAY
- [ ] Deuteronomy 33
- [ ] Deuteronomy 34
- [ ] Joshua 1
- [ ] Joshua 2
- [ ] Joshua 3

WEDNESDAY
- [ ] Joshua 4
- [ ] Joshua 5
- [ ] Joshua 6
- [ ] Joshua 7
- [ ] Joshua 8

THURSDAY
- [ ] Joshua 9
- [ ] Joshua 10
- [ ] Joshua 11
- [ ] Joshua 12
- [ ] Joshua 13

FRIDAY
- [ ] Joshua 14
- [ ] Joshua 15
- [ ] Joshua 16
- [ ] Joshua 17
- [ ] Joshua 18

SATURDAY
- [ ] Joshua 19
- [ ] Joshua 20
- [ ] Joshua 21
- [ ] Joshua 22
- [ ] Joshua 23

MONDAY
- [ ] Luke 7
- [ ] Luke 8

TUESDAY
- [ ] Luke 9
- [ ] Luke 10

WEDNESDAY
- [ ] Luke 11
- [ ] Luke 12

THURSDAY
- [ ] Luke 13
- [ ] Luke 14

FRIDAY
- [ ] Luke 15
- [ ] Luke 16

MONDAY
- [ ] Psalm 9:9-10
- [ ] Luke 12:25-26

TUESDAY
- [ ] 1 Chronicles 16:11
- [ ] Philippians 4:6

WEDNESDAY
- [ ] Deuteronomy 31:8
- [ ] John 14:27

THURSDAY
- [ ] Psalm 34:17
- [ ] 1 Peter 5:7

FRIDAY
- [ ] Joshua 1:9
- [ ] 2 Timothy 1:7

Growing Panes

When Christians say that the Bible is inspired, they are saying that it is "God-breathed." The Bible says "All Scripture is inspired by God and profitable for teaching, for reproof, for correction, for training in righteousness; that the man of God may be adequate, equipped for every good work." (2 Tim. 3:16-17) The word for "inspired" is the Greek qeovpneustos, "theopneustos," which means "God-breathed." In other words, this means that the Scriptures are authored from God, and that God moved through the personality and abilities of the biblical writers in such a way that what they wrote was without error and was correct in everything that it addressed. Therefore, the Scriptures are the product of both God and man.

This process of inspiration was not a mechanical dictation where the writer simply wrote down what was heard. Instead, the writers of the Bible were free to write what they wanted, the way they wanted, and when they wanted; yet it was God moving through them to ensure the integrity and accuracy of what was said.

The final product from this inspiration process, the Bible, was exactly what God intended. Yet, end results reflected the writer's personality and writing style.

1ST BIBLE READING MARATHON - **The Bible: From Darkness to The Light**

WEEK 7

JOSHUA 24-1 SAMUEL 30   **WEEK 7**   LUKE 17-JOHN 2

FAST TRACK
Old Testament Readings

SUNDAY
- [ ] Joshua 24
- [ ] Ruth 1
- [ ] Ruth 2
- [ ] Ruth 3
- [ ] Ruth 4

MONDAY
- [ ] 1 Samuel 1
- [ ] 1 Samuel 2
- [ ] 1 Samuel 3
- [ ] 1 Samuel 4
- [ ] 1 Samuel 5

TUESDAY
- [ ] 1 Samuel 6
- [ ] 1 Samuel 7
- [ ] 1 Samuel 8
- [ ] 1 Samuel 9
- [ ] 1 Samuel 10

WEDNESDAY
- [ ] 1 Samuel 11
- [ ] 1 Samuel 12
- [ ] 1 Samuel 13
- [ ] 1 Samuel 14
- [ ] 1 Samuel 15

THURSDAY
- [ ] 1 Samuel 16
- [ ] 1 Samuel 17
- [ ] 1 Samuel 18
- [ ] 1 Samuel 19
- [ ] 1 Samuel 20

FRIDAY
- [ ] 1 Samuel 21
- [ ] 1 Samuel 22
- [ ] 1 Samuel 23
- [ ] 1 Samuel 24
- [ ] 1 Samuel 25

SATURDAY
- [ ] 1 Samuel 26
- [ ] 1 Samuel 27
- [ ] 1 Samuel 28
- [ ] 1 Samuel 29
- [ ] 1 Samuel 30

MIDDLE LANES
New Testament Readings

MONDAY
- [ ] Luke 17
- [ ] Luke 18

TUESDAY
- [ ] Luke 19
- [ ] Luke 20

WEDNESDAY
- [ ] Luke 21
- [ ] Luke 22

THURSDAY
- [ ] Luke 23
- [ ] Luke 24

FRIDAY
- [ ] John 1
- [ ] John 2

INSIDE TRACK
Favorite Readings Old & New Testaments

MONDAY
- [ ] Psalm 46:10
- [ ] 2 Thessalonians 3:16

TUESDAY
- [ ] Ruth 1:16-17
- [ ] Hebrews 11:1

WEDNESDAY
- [ ] 1 Samuel 10:19-24
- [ ] John 8:24

THURSDAY
- [ ] 1 Samuel 15:17-23
- [ ] Romans 10:17

FRIDAY
- [ ] 1 Samuel 17:32-37
- [ ] Mark 5:36

NOTES

JESUS' VIEW OF THE OLD TESTAMENT

Growing Panes

Mark 12:35-36

And Jesus answering began to say, as He taught in the temple, "How is it that the scribes say that the Christ is the son of David? David himself said *in the Holy Spirit*, 'THE LORD SAID TO MY LORD, "SIT AT MY RIGHT HAND, UNTIL I PUT THINE ENEMIES BENEATH THY FEET."

Matthew 5:17-18

"Do not think that I came to abolish the Law or the Prophets; I did not come to abolish, but to fulfill. For truly I say to you, until heaven and earth pass away, not the smallest letter or stroke shall pass away from the Law, *until all is accomplished."*

Luke 16:28-31

"'I have five brothers – that he may warn them, lest they also come to this place of torment.' But Abraham said, *'They have Moses and the Prophets;* let them hear them.' But he said, 'No, Father Abraham, but if someone goes to them from the dead, they will repent!' But he said to him, *'If they do not listen to Moses and the Prophets,* neither will they be persuaded if someone rises from the dead.'"

1ST BIBLE READING MARATHON - The Bible: From Darkness to The Light

WEEK 8

FAST TRACK
Old Testament Readings

SUNDAY
- [ ] 1 Samuel 31
- [ ] 2 Samuel 1
- [ ] 2 Samuel 2
- [ ] 2 Samuel 3
- [ ] 2 Samuel 4

MONDAY
- [ ] 2 Samuel 5
- [ ] 2 Samuel 6
- [ ] 2 Samuel 7
- [ ] 2 Samuel 8
- [ ] 2 Samuel 9

TUESDAY
- [ ] 2 Samuel 10
- [ ] 2 Samuel 11
- [ ] 2 Samuel 12
- [ ] 2 Samuel 13
- [ ] 2 Samuel 14

WEDNESDAY
- [ ] 2 Samuel 15
- [ ] 2 Samuel 16
- [ ] 2 Samuel 17
- [ ] 2 Samuel 18
- [ ] 2 Samuel 19

THURSDAY
- [ ] 2 Samuel 20
- [ ] 2 Samuel 21
- [ ] 2 Samuel 22
- [ ] 2 Samuel 23
- [ ] 2 Samuel 24

FRIDAY
- [ ] 1 Kings 1
- [ ] 1 Kings 2
- [ ] 1 Kings 3
- [ ] 1 Kings 4
- [ ] 1 Kings 5

SATURDAY
- [ ] 1 Kings 6
- [ ] 1 Kings 7
- [ ] 1 Kings 8
- [ ] 1 Kings 9
- [ ] 1 Kings 10

MIDDLE LANES
New Testament Readings

MONDAY
- [ ] John 3
- [ ] John 4

TUESDAY
- [ ] John 5
- [ ] John 6

WEDNESDAY
- [ ] John 7
- [ ] John 8

THURSDAY
- [ ] John 9
- [ ] John 10

FRIDAY
- [ ] John 11
- [ ] John 12

INSIDE TRACK
Favorite Readings Old & New Testaments

MONDAY
- [ ] 2 Samuel 6:5-11
- [ ] Romans 10:9

TUESDAY
- [ ] 2 Samuel 12:1-7
- [ ] Hebrews 11:6

WEDNESDAY
- [ ] 2 Samuel 18:9-10
- [ ] 1 Corinthians 2:5

THURSDAY
- [ ] 2 Samuel 21:20:21
- [ ] Luke 1:37

FRIDAY
- [ ] 2 Samuel 22:1-4
- [ ] 1 Corinthians 16:13

NOTES

JESUS TAUGHT THAT MOSES' WRITINGS ARE TO BE BELIEVED

Growing Panes

John 5:39-47

"You search the Scriptures, because you think that in them you have eternal life; and *it is these that bear witness of Me*; and you are unwilling to come to Me, that you may have life. I do not receive glory from men; but I know you, that you do not have the love of God in yourselves.

I have come in My Father's name, and you do not receive Me; if another shall come in his own name, you will receive him. How can you believe, when you receive glory from one another, and you do not seek the glory that is from the *one and* only God?

Do not think that I will accuse you before the Father; the one who accuses you is Moses, in whom you have set your hope. *For if you believed Moses, you would believe Me; for he wrote of Me. But if you do not believe his writings, how will you believe My words*?"

Matthew 23:1-3

Then Jesus spoke to the multitudes and to His disciples, saying, "The scribes and the Pharisees have seated themselves in *the chair of Moses*; therefore *all that they tell you, do and observe*, but do not do according to their deeds; for they say things, and do not do them."

1ST BIBLE READING MARATHON - The Bible: From Darkness to The Light

WEEK 9

FAST TRACK

Old Testament Readings

SUNDAY
- [ ] 1 Kings 11
- [ ] 1 Kings 12
- [ ] 1 Kings 13
- [ ] 1 Kings 14
- [ ] 1 Kings 15

MONDAY
- [ ] 1 Kings 16
- [ ] 1 Kings 17
- [ ] 1 Kings 18
- [ ] 1 Kings 19
- [ ] 1 Kings 20

TUESDAY
- [ ] 1 Kings 21
- [ ] 1 Kings 22
- [ ] 2 Kings 1
- [ ] 2 Kings 2
- [ ] 2 Kings 3

WEDNESDAY
- [ ] 2 Kings 4
- [ ] 2 Kings 5
- [ ] 2 Kings 6
- [ ] 2 Kings 7
- [ ] 2 Kings 8

THURSDAY
- [ ] 2 Kings 9
- [ ] 2 Kings 10
- [ ] 2 Kings 11
- [ ] 2 Kings 12
- [ ] 2 Kings 13

FRIDAY
- [ ] 2 Kings 14
- [ ] 2 Kings 15
- [ ] 2 Kings 16
- [ ] 2 Kings 17
- [ ] 2 Kings 18

SATURDAY
- [ ] 2 Kings 19
- [ ] 2 Kings 20
- [ ] 2 Kings 21
- [ ] 2 Kings 22
- [ ] 2 Kings 23

MIDDLE LANES

New Testament Readings

MONDAY
- [ ] John 13
- [ ] John 14

TUESDAY
- [ ] John 15
- [ ] John 16

WEDNESDAY
- [ ] John 17
- [ ] John 18

THURSDAY
- [ ] John 19
- [ ] John 20

FRIDAY
- [ ] John 21
- [ ] Acts 1

INSIDE TRACK

Favorite Readings Old & New Testaments

MONDAY
- [ ] Psalm 119:30
- [ ] James 1:5-6

TUESDAY
- [ ] Psalm 86:15
- [ ] Ephesians 2:8-9

WEDNESDAY
- [ ] Psalm 33:22
- [ ] Galatians 2:20

THURSDAY
- [ ] Deuteronomy 31:6
- [ ] John 15:9-12

FRIDAY
- [ ] Proverbs 3:5-6
- [ ] 1 Corinthians 13:13

NOTES

JESUS' MINISTRY IS FULFILLMENT OF THE OLD TESTAMENT

Growing Panes

Luke 4:16-21

And He came to Nazareth, where He had been brought up; and as was His custom, He entered the synagogue on the Sabbath, and stood up to read. And the book of the prophet Isaiah was handed to Him. And He opened the book, and found the place where it was written, "THE SPIRIT OF THE LORD IS UPON ME, BECAUSE HE ANOINTED ME TO PREACH THE GOSPEL TO THE POOR. HE HAS SENT ME TO PROCLAIM RELEASE TO THE CAPTIVES, AND RECOVERY OF SIGHT TO THE BLIND, TO SET FREE THOSE WHO ARE DOWN-TRODDEN, TO PROCLAIM THE FAVORABLE YEAR OF THE LORD." And He closed the book, and gave it back to the attendant, and sat down; and the eyes of all in the synagogue were fixed upon Him. And He began to say to them, "Today this Scripture has been fulfilled in your hearing."

Mark 14:21; John 3:18

"For the Son of Man *is to* go, *just as it is written of Him*; but woe to that man by whom the Son of Man is betrayed! It would have been good for that man if he had not been born."

"I do not speak of all of you. I know the ones I have chosen; but it is that the Scripture may be fulfilled, 'HE WHO EATS MY BREAD HAS LIFTED UP HIS HEEL AGAINST ME.'"

WEEK 10

2 KINGS 24-2 CHRONICLES 4   **ACTS 3-11**

FAST TRACK
Old Testament Readings

SUNDAY
- [ ] 2 Kings 24
- [ ] 2 Kings 25
- [ ] 1 Chronicles 1
- [ ] 1 Chronicles 2
- [ ] 1 Chronicles 3

MONDAY
- [ ] 1 Chronicles 4
- [ ] 1 Chronicles 5
- [ ] 1 Chronicles 6
- [ ] 1 Chronicles 7
- [ ] 1 Chronicles 8

TUESDAY
- [ ] 1 Chronicles 9
- [ ] 1 Chronicles 10
- [ ] 1 Chronicles 11
- [ ] 1 Chronicles 12
- [ ] 1 Chronicles 13

WEDNESDAY
- [ ] 1 Chronicles 14
- [ ] 1 Chronicles 15
- [ ] 1 Chronicles 16
- [ ] 1 Chronicles 17
- [ ] 1 Chronicles 18

THURSDAY
- [ ] 1 Chronicles 19
- [ ] 1 Chronicles 20
- [ ] 1 Chronicles 21
- [ ] 1 Chronicles 22
- [ ] 1 Chronicles 23

FRIDAY
- [ ] 1 Chronicles 24
- [ ] 1 Chronicles 25
- [ ] 1 Chronicles 26
- [ ] 1 Chronicles 27
- [ ] 1 Chronicles 28

SATURDAY
- [ ] 1 Chronicles 29
- [ ] 2 Chronicles 1
- [ ] 2 Chronicles 2
- [ ] 2 Chronicles 3
- [ ] 2 Chronicles 4

MIDDLE LANES
New Testament Readings

MONDAY
- [ ] Acts 2
- [ ] Acts 3

TUESDAY
- [ ] Acts 4
- [ ] Acts 5

WEDNESDAY
- [ ] Acts 6
- [ ] Acts 7

THURSDAY
- [ ] Acts 8
- [ ] Acts 9

FRIDAY
- [ ] Acts 10
- [ ] Acts 11

INSIDE TRACK
Favorite Readings Old & New Testaments

MONDAY
- [ ] Psalm 120:1
- [ ] Philippians 4:13

TUESDAY
- [ ] Proverbs 23:18
- [ ] 1 Peter 1:6-7

WEDNESDAY
- [ ] Isaiah 41:10
- [ ] 1 Corinthians 2:3-5

THURSDAY
- [ ] 1 Chronicles 10:13-14
- [ ] Luke 17:5

FRIDAY
- [ ] 1 Chronicles 13:8-14
- [ ] Mark 9:24

NOTES

THE APOSTLES CHARGED WITH AUTHORITY

Acts 1:1-4

"The first account I composed, Theophilus, about all that Jesus began to do and teach, until the day when He was taken up, after He had by the Holy Spirit given orders to the apostles whom He had chosen. To these He also presented Himself alive, after His suffering, by many convincing proofs, appearing to them over a period of forty days, and speaking of the things concerning the kingdom of God. And gathering them together, He commanded them not to leave Jerusalem, but to wait for what the Father had promised, "Which," He said, "you heard of from Me."

Ephesians 2:19-20

So then you are no longer strangers and aliens, but you are fellow citizens with the saints, and are of God's household, having been built upon the foundation of the apostles and prophets, Christ Jesus Himself being the corner stone.

Acts 5:12

And at the hands of the apostles many signs and wonders were taking place among the people; and they were all with one accord in Solomon's portico.

1ST BIBLE READING MARATHON - The Bible: From Darkness to The Light

FAST TRACK
Old Testament Readings

2 CHRONICLES 5-EZRA 3 WEEK 11 ACTS 12-21

MIDDLE LANES
New Testament Readings

INSIDE TRACK
Favorite Readings Old & New Testaments

NOTES

SUNDAY
- [ ] 2 Chronicles 5
- [ ] 2 Chronicles 6
- [ ] 2 Chronicles 7
- [ ] 2 Chronicles 8
- [ ] 2 Chronicles 9

MONDAY
- [ ] 2 Chronicles 10
- [ ] 2 Chronicles 11
- [ ] 2 Chronicles 12
- [ ] 2 Chronicles 13
- [ ] 2 Chronicles 14

TUESDAY
- [ ] 2 Chronicles 15
- [ ] 2 Chronicles 16
- [ ] 2 Chronicles 17
- [ ] 2 Chronicles 18
- [ ] 2 Chronicles 19

WEDNESDAY
- [ ] 2 Chronicles 20
- [ ] 2 Chronicles 21
- [ ] 2 Chronicles 22
- [ ] 2 Chronicles 23
- [ ] 2 Chronicles 24

THURSDAY
- [ ] 2 Chronicles 25
- [ ] 2 Chronicles 26
- [ ] 2 Chronicles 27
- [ ] 2 Chronicles 28
- [ ] 2 Chronicles 29

FRIDAY
- [ ] 2 Chronicles 30
- [ ] 2 Chronicles 31
- [ ] 2 Chronicles 32
- [ ] 2 Chronicles 33
- [ ] 2 Chronicles 34

SATURDAY
- [ ] 2 Chronicles 35
- [ ] 2 Chronicles 36
- [ ] Ezra 1
- [ ] Ezra 2
- [ ] Ezra 3

MIDDLE LANES

MONDAY
- [ ] Acts 12
- [ ] Acts 13

TUESDAY
- [ ] Acts 14
- [ ] Acts 15

WEDNESDAY
- [ ] Acts 16
- [ ] Acts 17

THURSDAY
- [ ] Acts 18
- [ ] Acts 19

FRIDAY
- [ ] Acts 20
- [ ] Acts 21

INSIDE TRACK

MONDAY
- [ ] Job 36:11
- [ ] James 1:2-4

TUESDAY
- [ ] Proverbs 19:23
- [ ] 2 Corinthians 1:3-4

WEDNESDAY
- [ ] Proverbs 30: 7-9
- [ ] James 2:14-26

THURSDAY
- [ ] Proverbs 14:30
- [ ] 2 Timothy 4:7

FRIDAY
- [ ] Isaiah 46:4
- [ ] 1 Thessalonians 1:3

The Power of the Apostles with Signs and Wonders

Growing Panes

Acts 2:42-47

They devoted themselves to the apostles' teaching and to the fellowship, to the breaking of bread and to prayer. A sense of awe *came over everyone, and the apostles performed many wonders and signs.*

All the believers were together and had everything in common. Selling their possessions and goods, they shared with anyone who was in need.

With one accord they continued to meet daily in the temple courts and to break bread from house to house, sharing their meals with gladness and sincerity of heart, praising God and enjoying the favor of all the people. And the Lord added to their number daily those who were being saved..

Acts 14:3

Therefore they spent a long time there speaking boldly with reliance upon the Lord, who was bearing witness to the word of His grace, granting that signs and wonders be done by their hands.

FAST TRACK
Old Testament Readings

WEEK 12

EZRA 4-JOB 5

ACTS 22-ROMANS 3

NOTES

MIDDLE LANES
New Testament Readings

INSIDE TRACK
Favorite Readings Old & New Testaments

SUNDAY
- [ ] Ezra 4
- [ ] Ezra 5
- [ ] Ezra 6
- [ ] Ezra 7
- [ ] Ezra 8

MONDAY
- [ ] Ezra 9
- [ ] Ezra 10
- [ ] Nehemiah 1
- [ ] Nehemiah 2
- [ ] Nehemiah 3

TUESDAY
- [ ] Nehemiah 4
- [ ] Nehemiah 5
- [ ] Nehemiah 6
- [ ] Nehemiah 7
- [ ] Nehemiah 8

WEDNESDAY
- [ ] Nehemiah 9
- [ ] Nehemiah 10
- [ ] Nehemiah 11
- [ ] Nehemiah 12
- [ ] Nehemiah 13

THURSDAY
- [ ] Esther 1
- [ ] Esther 2
- [ ] Esther 3
- [ ] Esther 4
- [ ] Esther 5

FRIDAY
- [ ] Esther 6
- [ ] Esther 7
- [ ] Esther 8
- [ ] Esther 9
- [ ] Esther 10

SATURDAY
- [ ] Job 1
- [ ] Job 2
- [ ] Job 3
- [ ] Job 4
- [ ] Job 5

MONDAY
- [ ] Acts 22
- [ ] Acts 23

TUESDAY
- [ ] Acts 24
- [ ] Acts 25

WEDNESDAY
- [ ] Acts 26
- [ ] Acts 27

THURSDAY
- [ ] Acts 28
- [ ] Romans 1

FRIDAY
- [ ] Romans 2
- [ ] Romans 3

MONDAY
- [ ] Ezra 3:11
- [ ] Acts 22:16

TUESDAY
- [ ] Nehemiah 6:15-16
- [ ] Acts 23:6

WEDNESDAY
- [ ] Nehemiah 8:1-3
- [ ] Acts 27:23-24

THURSDAY
- [ ] Nehemiah 9:1-3
- [ ] Romans 1:16

FRIDAY
- [ ] Nehemiah 13:1-3
- [ ] Romans 3:10-12

What the Bible means to me?

Growing Panes

The Holy Bible is by far the greatest collection of writings of all time! The reason, because through the Bible we come to know the one true God, the creator of all things, and his plan for our salvation for us. The Bible is *the* Word of God for our generation, and everyone before and after. The Bible is the inspired Word of God and without error in its original writing.

It has been copied from many ancient manuscripts (the originals are no longer extant), and translated into many languages and various versions. And most important of all, the Bible proclaims to us the Gospel of Jesus Christ; how he was born of a virgin, died on the cross and raised from the dead by the glory of His father.

The Bible is reliable and trustworthy as the full and final authority on all matters of faith and life. No other writings are similarly inspired by God.

Reading, studying and applying the teachings of Scripture is at the center of how we grow in the love of God; how we come to understand God and his plan of salvation more fully; and how we learn to live according to the saving gospel of Jesus Christ.

WEEK 13

JOB 6-40

ROMANS 4-13

FAST TRACK
Old Testament Readings

MIDDLE LANES
New Testament Readings

INSIDE TRACK
Favorite Readings Old & New Testaments

NOTES

FAST TRACK — Old Testament Readings

SUNDAY
- [ ] Job 6
- [ ] Job 7
- [ ] Job 8
- [ ] Job 9
- [ ] Job 10

MONDAY
- [ ] Job 11
- [ ] Job 12
- [ ] Job 13
- [ ] Job 14
- [ ] Job 15

TUESDAY
- [ ] Job 16
- [ ] Job 17
- [ ] Job 18
- [ ] Job 19
- [ ] Job 20

WEDNESDAY
- [ ] Job 21
- [ ] Job 22
- [ ] Job 23
- [ ] Job 24
- [ ] Job 25

THURSDAY
- [ ] Job 26
- [ ] Job 27
- [ ] Job 28
- [ ] Job 29
- [ ] Job 30

FRIDAY
- [ ] Job 31
- [ ] Job 32
- [ ] Job 33
- [ ] Job 34
- [ ] Job 35

SATURDAY
- [ ] Job 36
- [ ] Job 37
- [ ] Job 38
- [ ] Job 39
- [ ] Job 40

MIDDLE LANES — New Testament Readings

MONDAY
- [ ] Romans 4
- [ ] Romans 5

TUESDAY
- [ ] Romans 6
- [ ] Romans 7

WEDNESDAY
- [ ] Romans 8
- [ ] Romans 9

THURSDAY
- [ ] Romans 10
- [ ] Romans 11

FRIDAY
- [ ] Romans 12
- [ ] Romans 13

INSIDE TRACK — Favorite Readings

MONDAY
- [ ] Esther 4:14
- [ ] Romans 4:20-21

TUESDAY
- [ ] Job 1:21
- [ ] Romans 5:1

WEDNESDAY
- [ ] Job 13:15
- [ ] Romans 5:8

THURSDAY
- [ ] Job 37:23-24
- [ ] Romans 6:1-2

FRIDAY
- [ ] Job:38:1-7
- [ ] Romans 6:23

What others think about the Bible...

Young man, my advice to you is that you cultivate an acquaintance with and firm belief in the Holy Scriptures, for this is your certain interest. I think Christ's system of morals and religion, as He left them with us, is the best the world ever saw or is likely to see.

— BENJAMIN FRANKLIN

I have said and always will say that the studious perusal of the sacred volume will make better citizens, better fathers, and better husbands.

— THOMAS JEFFERSON

Jesus is the most perfect of all men that have yet appeared.

— RALPH WALDO EMERSON

1ST BIBLE READING MARATHON - **The Bible: From Darkness to The Light**

FAST TRACK
Old Testament Readings

WEEK 14

MIDDLE LANES
New Testament Readings

INSIDE TRACK
Favorite Readings Old & New Testaments

NOTES

FAST TRACK (Old Testament Readings)

SUNDAY
- [ ] Job 41
- [ ] Job 42
- [ ] Psalm 1
- [ ] Psalm 2
- [ ] Psalm 3

MONDAY
- [ ] Psalm 4
- [ ] Psalm 5
- [ ] Psalm 6
- [ ] Psalm 7
- [ ] Psalm 8

TUESDAY
- [ ] Psalm 9
- [ ] Psalm 10
- [ ] Psalm 11
- [ ] Psalm 12
- [ ] Psalm 13

WEDNESDAY
- [ ] Psalm 14
- [ ] Psalm 15
- [ ] Psalm 16
- [ ] Psalm 17
- [ ] Psalm 18

THURSDAY
- [ ] Psalm 19
- [ ] Psalm 20
- [ ] Psalm 21
- [ ] Psalm 22
- [ ] Psalm 23

FRIDAY
- [ ] Psalm 24
- [ ] Psalm 25
- [ ] Psalm 26
- [ ] Psalm 27
- [ ] Psalm 28

SATURDAY
- [ ] Psalm 29
- [ ] Psalm 30
- [ ] Psalm 31
- [ ] Psalm 32
- [ ] Psalm 33

MIDDLE LANES (New Testament Readings)

MONDAY
- [ ] Romans 14
- [ ] Romans 15

TUESDAY
- [ ] Romans 16
- [ ] 1 Corinthians 1

WEDNESDAY
- [ ] 1 Corinthians 2
- [ ] 1 Corinthians 3

THURSDAY
- [ ] 1 Corinthians 4
- [ ] 1 Corinthians 5

FRIDAY
- [ ] 1 Corinthians 6
- [ ] 1 Corinthians 7

INSIDE TRACK (Favorite Readings Old & New Testaments)

MONDAY
- [ ] Psalm 1:1-6
- [ ] Romans 8:1

TUESDAY
- [ ] Psalm 15:1-5
- [ ] Romans 8:38-39

WEDNESDAY
- [ ] Psalm 19:1-14
- [ ] Romans 10:17

THURSDAY
- [ ] Psalm 23:1-6
- [ ] Romans 12:1-2

FRIDAY
- [ ] Psalm 29:1-2
- [ ] Romans 16:17-18

What others think about the Bible...

If we abide by the principles taught in the Bible, our country will go on prospering and to prosper; but, if we and our posterity neglect its instructions and authority, no man can tell how sudden a catastrophe may overwhelm us and bury all our glory in profound obscurity. The Bible is the book of all others for lawyers as well as divines, and I pity the man who cannot find in it a rich supply of thought and rule of conduct. I believe Jesus Christ to be the Son of God. The miracles which He wrought establish in my mind His personal authority and render it proper for me to believe what He asserts.

- DANIEL WEBSTER

The Growing Panes

FAST TRACK
Old Testament Readings

SUNDAY
- [ ] Psalm 34
- [ ] Psalm 35
- [ ] Psalm 36
- [ ] Psalm 37
- [ ] Psalm 38

MONDAY
- [ ] Psalm 39
- [ ] Psalm 40
- [ ] Psalm 41
- [ ] Psalm 42
- [ ] Psalm 43

TUESDAY
- [ ] Psalm 44
- [ ] Psalm 45
- [ ] Psalm 46
- [ ] Psalm 47
- [ ] Psalm 48

WEDNESDAY
- [ ] Psalm 49
- [ ] Psalm 50
- [ ] Psalm 51
- [ ] Psalm 52
- [ ] Psalm 53

THURSDAY
- [ ] Psalm 54
- [ ] Psalm 55
- [ ] Psalm 56
- [ ] Psalm 57
- [ ] Psalm 58

FRIDAY
- [ ] Psalm 59
- [ ] Psalm 60
- [ ] Psalm 61
- [ ] Psalm 62
- [ ] Psalm 63

SATURDAY
- [ ] Psalm 64
- [ ] Psalm 65
- [ ] Psalm 66
- [ ] Psalm 67
- [ ] Psalm 68

PSALM 34-68   **WEEK 15**   1 CORINTHIANS 8-2 CORINTHIANS 1

MIDDLE LANES
New Testament Readings

MONDAY
- [ ] 1 Corinthians 8
- [ ] 1 Corinthians 9

TUESDAY
- [ ] 1 Corinthians 10
- [ ] 1 Corinthians 11

WEDNESDAY
- [ ] 1 Corinthians 12
- [ ] 1 Corinthians 13

THURSDAY
- [ ] 1 Corinthians 14
- [ ] 1 Corinthians 15

FRIDAY
- [ ] 1 Corinthians 16
- [ ] 2 Corinthians 1

INSIDE TRACK
Favorite Readings Old & New Testaments

MONDAY
- [ ] Psalm 37:1-8
- [ ] 1 Corinthians 1:18

TUESDAY
- [ ] Psalm 37:23-26
- [ ] 1 Corinthians 3:16

WEDNESDAY
- [ ] Psalm 42:1-2
- [ ] 1 Corinthians 6:20

THURSDAY
- [ ] Psalm 51:1-2
- [ ] 1 Corinthians 10:13

FRIDAY
- [ ] Psalm 51:7-11
- [ ] 1 Corinthians 15:3

NOTES

What others think about the Bible...

This book contains the mind of God, the state of man, the way of salvation, the doom of sinners, and the happiness of believers. Its doctrine is holy, its precepts are binding, its histories are true, and its decisions are immutable. Read it to be wise, believe in it to be safe, and practice it to be holy. It contains light to direct you, food to support you, and comfort to cheer you. It is the traveler's map, the pilgrim's staff, the pilot's compass, the soldier's sword, and the Christian's charter. Here paradise is restored, heaven opened, and the gates of hell disclosed. Christ is its grand object, our good its design, and the glory of God its end. It should fill the memory, rule the heart, and guide the feet. Read it slowly, frequently, and prayerfully. It is a mine of wealth, a paradise of glory, and a river of pleasure. It is given you in life, will be opened in the judgment, and be remembered forever. It involves the highest responsibility, will reward the greatest labor, and will condemn all who trifle with its sacred contents.

- Unknown

FAST TRACK

Old Testament Readings

MIDDLE LANES

New Testament Readings

INSIDE TRACK

Favorite Readings Old & New Testaments

NOTES

SUNDAY
- ☐ Psalm 69
- ☐ Psalm 70
- ☐ Psalm 71
- ☐ Psalm 72
- ☐ Psalm 73

MONDAY
- ☐ Psalm 74
- ☐ Psalm 75
- ☐ Psalm 76
- ☐ Psalm 77
- ☐ Psalm 78

TUESDAY
- ☐ Psalm 79
- ☐ Psalm 80
- ☐ Psalm 81
- ☐ Psalm 82
- ☐ Psalm 83

WEDNESDAY
- ☐ Psalm 84
- ☐ Psalm 85
- ☐ Psalm 86
- ☐ Psalm 87
- ☐ Psalm 88

THURSDAY
- ☐ Psalm 89
- ☐ Psalm 90
- ☐ Psalm 91
- ☐ Psalm 92
- ☐ Psalm 93

FRIDAY
- ☐ Psalm 94
- ☐ Psalm 95
- ☐ Psalm 96
- ☐ Psalm 97
- ☐ Psalm 98

SATURDAY
- ☐ Psalm 99
- ☐ Psalm 100
- ☐ Psalm 101
- ☐ Psalm 102
- ☐ Psalm 103

MONDAY (Middle Lanes)
- ☐ 2 Corinthians 2
- ☐ 2 Corinthians 3

TUESDAY (Middle Lanes)
- ☐ 2 Corinthians 4
- ☐ 2 Corinthians 5

WEDNESDAY (Middle Lanes)
- ☐ 2 Corinthians 6
- ☐ 2 Corinthians 7

THURSDAY (Middle Lanes)
- ☐ 2 Corinthians 8
- ☐ 2 Corinthians 9

FRIDAY (Middle Lanes)
- ☐ 2 Corinthians 10
- ☐ 2 Corinthians 11

MONDAY (Inside Track)
- ☐ Psalm 85:10-11
- ☐ 1 Corinthians 15:58

TUESDAY (Inside Track)
- ☐ Psalm 27:4
- ☐ 2 Corinthians 5:17

WEDNESDAY (Inside Track)
- ☐ Psalm 34:18
- ☐ 2 Corinthians 6:14

THURSDAY (Inside Track)
- ☐ Psalm 37:4
- ☐ 2 Corinthians 9:6-7

FRIDAY (Inside Track)
- ☐ Psalm 55:22
- ☐ 2 Corinthians 4:5

God has given us His instruction manual for daily living, so every time you need an answer to a question or just an uplifting word; the Bible is there to comfort and assure you that all is well. I encourage you to go to the Book that can calm your fears and show you that no matter how hopeless your situation may be, there is still One who says "With men it may be impossible, but with God all things are possible." (Matthew 19:26)

Whatever the problem or whatever has you worried, God's Word has the answer of freedom and comfort. Open the Bible if you have not done so recently and ask the Lord to speak to you through His Word and God will be faithful to hear and answer your prayer and calm every fear in your heart; for in Him there is only Peace and Joy unspeakable. (Psalm 16:11)

"My son, give attention to my words; Incline your ear to my sayings. Do not let them depart from your eyes; Keep them in the midst of your heart; For they are life to those who find them, And health to all their flesh." (Proverbs 4:20-22)

Growing Panes

1ST BIBLE READING MARATHON - The Bible: From Darkness to The Light

FAST TRACK
Old Testament Readings

PSALM 104-138

WEEK 17

2 CORINTHIANS 12-COLOSSIANS 2

MIDDLE LANES
New Testament Readings

INSIDE TRACK
Favorite Readings Old and New Testaments

NOTES

SUNDAY
- [ ] Psalm 104
- [ ] Psalm 105
- [ ] Psalm 106
- [ ] Psalm 107
- [ ] Psalm 108

MONDAY
- [ ] Psalm 109
- [ ] Psalm 110
- [ ] Psalm 111
- [ ] Psalm 112
- [ ] Psalm 113

TUESDAY
- [ ] Psalm 114
- [ ] Psalm 115
- [ ] Psalm 116
- [ ] Psalm 117
- [ ] Psalm 118

WEDNESDAY
- [ ] Psalm 119
- [ ] Psalm 120
- [ ] Psalm 121
- [ ] Psalm 122
- [ ] Psalm 123

THURSDAY
- [ ] Psalm 124
- [ ] Psalm 125
- [ ] Psalm 126
- [ ] Psalm 127
- [ ] Psalm 128

FRIDAY
- [ ] Psalm 129
- [ ] Psalm 130
- [ ] Psalm 131
- [ ] Psalm 132
- [ ] Psalm 133

SATURDAY
- [ ] Psalm 134
- [ ] Psalm 135
- [ ] Psalm 136
- [ ] Psalm 137
- [ ] Psalm 138

New Testament Readings

MONDAY
- [ ] 2 Corinthians 12
- [ ] 2 Corinthians 13

TUESDAY
- [ ] Galatians 1
- [ ] Galatians 2

WEDNESDAY
- [ ] Galatians 3
- [ ] Galatians 4

THURSDAY
- [ ] Galatians 5
- [ ] Galatians 6

FRIDAY
- [ ] Ephesians 1
- [ ] Ephesians 2

Favorite Readings Old and New Testaments

MONDAY
- [ ] Psalm 119:28
- [ ] 2 Corinthians 13:5

TUESDAY
- [ ] Psalm 147:3
- [ ] Galatians 2:20

WEDNESDAY
- [ ] Psalm 127:3-5
- [ ] Galatians 5:22-23

THURSDAY
- [ ] Psalm 100
- [ ] Galatians 6:9-10

FRIDAY
- [ ] Psalm 121
- [ ] Ephesians 1:7

THE GOSSIPER

Growing Panes

A woman repeated a bit of gossip about a neighbor. Within a few days the whole community knew the story. The person it concerned was deeply hurt and offended. Later, the woman responsible for spreading the rumor learned that it was completely untrue. She was very sorry and went to a wise old sage to find out what she could do to repair the damage.

"Go to the marketplace," he said, "and purchase a chicken, and have it killed. Then on your way home, pluck its feathers and drop them one by one along the road." Although surprised by this advice, the woman did what she was told.

The next day the wise man said, "Now, go and collect all those feathers you dropped yesterday and bring them back to me."

The woman followed the same road, but to her dismay the wind had blown all the feathers away. After searching for hours, she returned with only three feathers in her hand.

"You see," said the old sage, "It's easy to drop them, but it is impossible to get them back. So it is with gossip. It doesn't take much to spread a rumor, but once you do you can never completely undo the wrong."

-Author Unknown

1ST BIBLE READING MARATHON - The Bible: From Darkness to The Light

FAST TRACK
Old Testament Readings

PSALM 139-PROVERBS 20 # WEEK 18 — EPHESIANS 3-COLOSSIANS 2

MIDDLE LANES
INSIDE TRACK

New Testament Readings

Favorite Readings Old & New Testaments

NOTES

SUNDAY
- [ ] Psalm 139
- [ ] Psalm 140
- [ ] Psalm 141
- [ ] Psalm 142
- [ ] Psalm 143

MONDAY
- [ ] Psalm 144
- [ ] Psalm 145
- [ ] Psalm 146
- [ ] Psalm 147
- [ ] Psalm 148

TUESDAY
- [ ] Psalm 149
- [ ] Psalm 150
- [ ]
- [ ]
- [ ]

WEDNESDAY
- [ ] Proverbs 1
- [ ] Proverbs 2
- [ ] Proverbs 3
- [ ] Proverbs 4
- [ ] Proverbs 5

THURSDAY
- [ ] Proverbs 6
- [ ] Proverbs 7
- [ ] Proverbs 8
- [ ] Proverbs 9
- [ ] Proverbs 10

FRIDAY
- [ ] Proverbs 11
- [ ] Proverbs 12
- [ ] Proverbs 13
- [ ] Proverbs 14
- [ ] Proverbs 15

SATURDAY
- [ ] Proverbs 16
- [ ] Proverbs 17
- [ ] Proverbs 18
- [ ] Proverbs 19
- [ ] Proverbs 20

MIDDLE LANES — New Testament Readings

MONDAY
- [ ] Ephesians 3
- [ ] Ephesians 4

TUESDAY
- [ ] Ephesians 5
- [ ] Ephesians 6

WEDNESDAY
- [ ] Philippians 1
- [ ] Philippians 2

THURSDAY
- [ ] Philippians 3
- [ ] Philippians 4

FRIDAY
- [ ] Colossians 1
- [ ] Colossians 2

INSIDE TRACK — Favorite Readings Old & New Testaments

MONDAY
- [ ] Psalm 139:1-6
- [ ] Ephesians 4:29

TUESDAY
- [ ] Psalm 139:14
- [ ] Ephesians 6:1-3

WEDNESDAY
- [ ] Psalm 139:23-24
- [ ] Philippians 2:14-15

THURSDAY
- [ ] Psalm 144:3-4
- [ ] Philippians 4:13

FRIDAY
- [ ] Psalm 149:1
- [ ] Colossians 3:16-17

A Letter from Hell...

One day a woman named Louise dreamed a very frightful dream. She dreamed that someone in Hell wrote a letter to her, and it was to be delivered to her by a messenger. The messenger gave her the letter, saying only that a friend had written it to her from Hell. Louise with trembling hands took the letter and read:

*My Friend I stand in Judgment now, And feel that you're somehow to blame. On earth, I walked with you day by day, and never did you point the Way to me. You knew the Lord, but **never** did you tell me His story. Though we lived together on the earth, you never told me of the second birth, and now, I stand this day condemned because you failed to mention Him to me. I called you "friend" and trusted you, but now I learn that it's too late, You could have kept me from this fate. We walked by day and talked by night, and yet you did not show me the light. You let me live, and love, and die. Yes, I called you a "friend" in life, And trusted you through joy and strife. And yet on coming to the end, I cannot, now, call you "My Friend."*

---Marsha

When she awoke, she contemplated the meaning of her dream. She realized that as a Christian, she failed in her duty to "Go out to all the world and preach the Gospel." She promised herself that the next day, she would call Marsha and invite her to church with her. So, the next morning she called Marsha. This was the conversation:

"Hello, Bill, Is Marsha there?"
"Louise, you don't know?"
"No, Bill, know what?"
"Marsha was killed last night in a car accident. I thought you knew!"

- Author Unknown

FAST TRACK
Old Testament Readings

SUNDAY
☐ Proverbs 21
☐ Proverbs 22
☐ Proverbs 23
☐ Proverbs 24
☐ Proverbs 25
MONDAY
☐ Proverbs 26
☐ Proverbs 27
☐ Proverbs 28
☐ Proverbs 29
☐ Proverbs 30
TUESDAY
☐ Proverbs 31
☐
☐
☐
☐
WEDNESDAY
☐ Ecclesiastes 1
☐ Ecclesiastes 2
☐ Ecclesiastes 3
☐ Ecclesiastes 4
☐ Ecclesiastes 5
THURSDAY
☐ Ecclesiastes 6
☐ Ecclesiastes 7
☐ Ecclesiastes 8
☐ Ecclesiastes 9
☐ Ecclesiastes 10
FRIDAY
☐ Ecclesiastes 11
☐ Ecclesiastes 12
☐
☐
☐
SATURDAY
☐ Song of Solomon 1
☐ Song of Solomon 2
☐ Song of Solomon 3
☐ Song of Solomon 4
☐ Song of Solomon 5

PROV 21-SONG OF SOL 5 **WEEK 19** **COLOSSIANS 3-2 THESSALONIANS 1**

MIDDLE LANES
New Testament Readings

MONDAY
- ☐ Colossians 3
- ☐ Colossians 4

TUESDAY
- ☐ 1 Thessalonians 1
- ☐ 1 Thessalonians 2

WEDNESDAY
- ☐ 1 Thessalonians 3
- ☐ 1 Thessalonians 4

THURSDAY
- ☐ 1 Thessalonians 5
- ☐

FRIDAY
- ☐ 2 Thessalonians 1
- ☐

INSIDE TRACK
Favorite Readings Old & New Testaments

MONDAY
- ☐ Proverbs 3:5
- ☐ Colossians 4:2

TUESDAY
- ☐ Proverbs 22:6
- ☐ 1 Thessalonians 5:16-18

WEDNESDAY
- ☐ Proverbs 1:7
- ☐ 1 Thessalonians 4:16-17

THURSDAY
- ☐ Proverbs 14:12
- ☐ 1 Thessalonians 5:1-2

FRIDAY
- ☐ Proverbs 27:17
- ☐ 2 Thessalonians 1:11-12

NOTES

Cooperation...

Evxn though my typxwritxr is an old modxl, it works quitx wxll xxcxpt for onx of the kxys. I havx many timxs wishxd that it workxd pxrfxctly. It is trux that thxrx arx forty-onx kxys that function wxll xnough, but just onx kxy not working makxs thx diffxrxncx.

Somxtimxs it sxxms to mx that our church is somxthing likx my typxwritxr --not all thx kxy pxoplx arx working propxrly. As onx of thxm, you may say to yoursxlf, "Wxll, I am only onx pxrson, I don't makx or brxak thx church." But it doxs makx a big diffxrxncx, bxcausx a church, to bx xffxctivx, nxxds thx activx participation of xvxry pxrson.

Thx nxxt timx you think your xfforts arx not nxxdxd vxry much, rxmxmbxr my typxwritxr and thx missing kxy and say to yoursxlf, "I am a kxy pxrson in thx congrxgation and I am vxry much nxxdxd." This is what happxns to thx wholx church at onx timx or anothxr, so nxnxr think your absxncx will go unnoticxd!

Remember this story and never allow yourself to be a broken key – but rather challenge yourself to be a useful one.

-Author Unknown

Growing Panes

FAST TRACK

Old Testament Readings

SONG OF SOL 6-ISAIAH 30 # WEEK 20 **2 Thessalonians 2-2 Timothy 2**

MIDDLE LANES

INSIDE TRACK

NOTES

SUNDAY
- [ ] Song of Solomon 6
- [ ] Song of Solomon 7
- [ ] Song of Solomon 8
- [ ]
- [ ]

MONDAY
- [ ] Isaiah 1
- [ ] Isaiah 2
- [ ] Isaiah 3
- [ ] Isaiah 4
- [ ] Isaiah 5

TUESDAY
- [ ] Isaiah 6
- [ ] Isaiah 7
- [ ] Isaiah 8
- [ ] Isaiah 9
- [ ] Isaiah 10

WEDNESDAY
- [ ] Isaiah 11
- [ ] Isaiah 12
- [ ] Isaiah 13
- [ ] Isaiah 14
- [ ] Isaiah 15

THURSDAY
- [ ] Isaiah 16
- [ ] Isaiah 17
- [ ] Isaiah 18
- [ ] Isaiah 19
- [ ] Isaiah 20

FRIDAY
- [ ] Isaiah 21
- [ ] Isaiah 22
- [ ] Isaiah 23
- [ ] Isaiah 24
- [ ] Isaiah 25

SATURDAY
- [ ] Isaiah 26
- [ ] Isaiah 27
- [ ] Isaiah 28
- [ ] Isaiah 29
- [ ] Isaiah 30

New Testament Readings

MONDAY
- [ ] 2 Thessalonians 2
- [ ] 2 Thessalonians 3

TUESDAY
- [ ] 1 Timothy 1
- [ ] 1 Timothy 2

WEDNESDAY
- [ ] 1 Timothy 3
- [ ] 1 Timothy 4

THURSDAY
- [ ] 1 Timothy 5
- [ ] 1 Timothy 6

FRIDAY
- [ ] 2 Timothy 1
- [ ] 2 Timothy 2

Favorite Readings Old & New Testaments

MONDAY
- [ ] Ecclesiastes 12:13
- [ ] 2 Thessalonians 2:15

TUESDAY
- [ ] Isaiah 9:6
- [ ] 1 Timothy 2:5

WEDNESDAY
- [ ] Isaiah 7:14
- [ ] 1 Timothy 4:12

THURSDAY
- [ ] Isaiah 40:31
- [ ] 1 Timothy 5:8

FRIDAY
- [ ] Isaiah 53:6
- [ ] 2 Timothy 2:15

THE ACORN AND THE PUMPKIN

Growing Panes

There is an old poem that tells the story of a woman who was walking through a meadow. As she strolled along meditating on nature, she came upon a field of golden pumpkins. In the corner of the field stood a majestic oak tree.

The woman, weary, sat down under the oak and began to muse about the strange twists in nature. Tiny acorns hung on huge branches and huge pumpkins sat on tiny vines. She thought, "God blundered with creation! He should have put the small acorns on the tiny vines and the large pumpkins on the huge branches."

Resting beneath the tree, she drifted off to sleep. She was awakened by a tiny acorn bouncing off her nose. Chuckling to herself, she amended her previous thought, "Just goes to show that God knew best all along!"

-Author Unknown

FAST TRACK
Old Testament Readings

| ISAIAH 31-65 | **WEEK 21** | 2 TIMOTHY 3-HEBREWS 4 |

MIDDLE LANES — New Testament Readings

INSIDE TRACK — Favorite Readings Old & New Testaments

NOTES

FAST TRACK — Old Testament Readings

SUNDAY
- ☐ Isaiah 31
- ☐ Isaiah 32
- ☐ Isaiah 33
- ☐ Isaiah 34
- ☐ Isaiah 35

MONDAY
- ☐ Isaiah 36
- ☐ Isaiah 37
- ☐ Isaiah 38
- ☐ Isaiah 39
- ☐ Isaiah 40

TUESDAY
- ☐ Isaiah 41
- ☐ Isaiah 42
- ☐ Isaiah 43
- ☐ Isaiah 44
- ☐ Isaiah 45

WEDNESDAY
- ☐ Isaiah 46
- ☐ Isaiah 47
- ☐ Isaiah 48
- ☐ Isaiah 49
- ☐ Isaiah 50

THURSDAY
- ☐ Isaiah 51
- ☐ Isaiah 52
- ☐ Isaiah 53
- ☐ Isaiah 54
- ☐ Isaiah 55

FRIDAY
- ☐ Isaiah 56
- ☐ Isaiah 57
- ☐ Isaiah 58
- ☐ Isaiah 59
- ☐ Isaiah 60

SATURDAY
- ☐ Isaiah 61
- ☐ Isaiah 62
- ☐ Isaiah 63
- ☐ Isaiah 64
- ☐ Isaiah 65

MIDDLE LANES — New Testament Readings

MONDAY
- ☐ 2 Timothy 3
- ☐ 2 Timothy 4

TUESDAY
- ☐ Titus 1
- ☐ Titus 2

WEDNESDAY
- ☐ Titus 3
- ☐ Philemon 1

THURSDAY
- ☐ Hebrews 1
- ☐ Hebrews 2

FRIDAY
- ☐ Hebrews 3
- ☐ Hebrews 4

INSIDE TRACK — Favorite Readings Old & New Testaments

MONDAY
- ☐ Isaiah 55:8
- ☐ 2 Timothy 3:16-17

TUESDAY
- ☐ Isaiah 1:18
- ☐ Titus 2:11-14

WEDNESDAY
- ☐ Isaiah 41:10
- ☐ Titus 3:5

THURSDAY
- ☐ Isaiah 59:1-2
- ☐ Hebrews 4:12

FRIDAY
- ☐ Isaiah 55:11
- ☐ Hebrews 10:24-25

SAVING THE BROKEN PIECES

Growing Panes

At the Royal Palace of Tehran in Iran, you can see one of the most beautiful mosaic works in the world. The ceilings and walls flash like diamonds with multifaceted reflections.

Originally, when the palace was designed, the architect specified huge sheets of mirrors on the walls. When the first shipment arrived from Paris, they found to their horror that the mirrors were shattered. The contractor threw them in the trash and brought the sad news to the architect.

Amazingly, the architect ordered all of the broken pieces collected, then smashed them into tiny pieces and glued them to the walls to become a mosaic of silvery, shimmering, mirrored bits of glass.

Broken to become beautiful! It's possible to turn your scars into stars. It's possible to be better because of the brokenness. It is extremely rare to find in the great museums of the world objects of antiquity that are unbroken. Indeed, some of the most precious pieces in the world are only fragments that remain a hallowed reminder of a glorious past.

Never underestimate God's power to repair and restore.

- Robert Schuller

FAST TRACK
Old Testament Readings

MIDDLE LANES
New Testament Readings

INSIDE TRACK
Favorite Readings Old & New Testaments

NOTES

SUNDAY
- [ ] Isaiah 66
- [ ]
- [ ]
- [ ]
- [ ]

MONDAY
- [ ] Lamentations 1
- [ ] Lamentations 2
- [ ] Lamentations 3
- [ ] Lamentations 4
- [ ] Lamentations 5

TUESDAY
- [ ] Ezekiel 1
- [ ] Ezekiel 2
- [ ] Ezekiel 3
- [ ] Ezekiel 4
- [ ] Ezekiel 5

WEDNESDAY
- [ ] Ezekiel 6
- [ ] Ezekiel 7
- [ ] Ezekiel 8
- [ ] Ezekiel 9
- [ ] Ezekiel 10

THURSDAY
- [ ] Ezekiel 11
- [ ] Ezekiel 12
- [ ] Ezekiel 13
- [ ] Ezekiel 14
- [ ] Ezekiel 15

FRIDAY
- [ ] Ezekiel 16
- [ ] Ezekiel 17
- [ ] Ezekiel 18
- [ ] Ezekiel 19
- [ ] Ezekiel 20

SATURDAY
- [ ] Ezekiel 21
- [ ] Ezekiel 22
- [ ] Ezekiel 23
- [ ] Ezekiel 24
- [ ] Ezekiel 25

MIDDLE LANES (New Testament Readings)

MONDAY
- [ ] Hebrews 5
- [ ] Hebrews 6

TUESDAY
- [ ] Hebrews 7
- [ ] Hebrews 8

WEDNESDAY
- [ ] Hebrews 9
- [ ] Hebrews 10

THURSDAY
- [ ] Hebrews 11
- [ ] Hebrews 12

FRIDAY
- [ ] Hebrews 13
- [ ] James 1

INSIDE TRACK

MONDAY
- [ ] Isaiah 2:1-2
- [ ] Hebrews 11:1

TUESDAY
- [ ] Lamentations 3:23
- [ ] Hebrews 11:6

WEDNESDAY
- [ ] Ezekiel 18:20
- [ ] Hebrews 13:5

THURSDAY
- [ ] Ezekiel 20:21
- [ ] Hebrews 13:17

FRIDAY
- [ ] Ezekiel 33:11
- [ ] James 1:2-4

Growing Panes

Paul Tournier was a brilliant thinker and writer, and an influential Christian therapist during his time. Doctors from around the world traveled to his home in Switzerland to learn from him. He wrote, "*It is a little embarrassing for students to come over and study my 'techniques.' They always go away disappointed, because all I do is accept people.*"

Accepting is not the same as approving, condoning, or even tolerating bad behavior. Acceptance is an act of the heart in which we recognize that, despite someone's behavior, he or she has value in God's sight, and we honor that. But this can be a hard thing to do! There are many ways to communicate acceptance to people. One of them is to listen to them with patience and compassion and receive them with love in the name of Jesus. Another is to refrain from condemnation and judgments, from constantly evaluating and analyzing. We must take captive those thoughts of condemnation toward others, and submit to God. As we draw near to Him, we ask Him to love through us.

"*Be devoted to one another in brotherly love. Honor one another above yourselves*" (Romans 12:10)

- Author Unknown

WEEK 23

FAST TRACK
Old Testament Readings

SUNDAY
- [ ] Ezekiel 26
- [ ] Ezekiel 27
- [ ] Ezekiel 28
- [ ] Ezekiel 29
- [ ] Ezekiel 30

MONDAY
- [ ] Ezekiel 31
- [ ] Ezekiel 32
- [ ] Ezekiel 33
- [ ] Ezekiel 34
- [ ] Ezekiel 35

TUESDAY
- [ ] Ezekiel 36
- [ ] Ezekiel 37
- [ ] Ezekiel 38
- [ ] Ezekiel 39
- [ ] Ezekiel 40

WEDNESDAY
- [ ] Ezekiel 41
- [ ] Ezekiel 42
- [ ] Ezekiel 43
- [ ] Ezekiel 44
- [ ] Ezekiel 45

THURSDAY
- [ ] Ezekiel 46
- [ ] Ezekiel 47
- [ ] Ezekiel 48
- [ ]
- [ ]

FRIDAY
- [ ] Daniel 1
- [ ] Daniel 2
- [ ] Daniel 3
- [ ] Daniel 4
- [ ] Daniel 5

SATURDAY
- [ ] Daniel 6
- [ ] Daniel 7
- [ ] Daniel 8
- [ ] Daniel 9
- [ ] Daniel 10

MIDDLE LANES
New Testament Readings

MONDAY
- [ ] James 2
- [ ] James 3

TUESDAY
- [ ] James 4
- [ ] James 5

WEDNESDAY
- [ ] 1 Peter 1
- [ ] 1 Peter 2

THURSDAY
- [ ] 1 Peter 3
- [ ] 1 Peter 5

FRIDAY
- [ ] 2 Peter 1
- [ ] 2 Peter 2

INSIDE TRACK
Favorite Readings Old & New Testaments

MONDAY
- [ ] Ezekiel 1:28
- [ ] James 1:22

TUESDAY
- [ ] Ezekiel 2:3
- [ ] James 4:17

WEDNESDAY
- [ ] Ezekiel 9:10
- [ ] 1 Peter 2:2

THURSDAY
- [ ] Ezekiel 11:12
- [ ] 1 Peter 4:14-16

FRIDAY
- [ ] Ezekiel 18:21
- [ ] 2 Peter 1:5-7

NOTES

A few years ago, a commercial on television began with a black and white clip of Lou Gehrig being honored by Yankee fans on his last day of play. His career was shortened by ALS, which is now called Lou Gehrig's disease, a debilitating muscle disease that eventually stops the heart. What would you have said in the face of this heartbreaking challenge? Amazingly, he begins: *Today I consider myself the luckiest man on the face of the earth."* How could he say that? Gratitude. Gratitude for all the gifts he had been given, for all the love he had been shown by fans, for all the opportunities he had. He focused on the joys not the losses. That's cultivating thankfulness!

Being thankful doesn't come easy for some of us, but God says to cultivate thankfulness. How do you cultivate anything? You work at it. You nourish it. You do whatever it takes to make it thrive. Gratitude comes from humility. *"A proud man is seldom a grateful man, for he never thinks he gets as much as he deserves"* (Henry Ward Beecher). God is good and merciful. The price that Christ paid so that you could be redeemed is immense. You truly are the luckiest person on the face of the earth.

"Let the peace of Christ rule in your hearts, since as members of one body you were called to peace. And be thankful!" (Colossians 3:15)

Growing Panes

FAST TRACK
Old Testament Readings

DANIEL 11-AMOS 9 | **WEEK 24** | 2 PETER 3-REVELATION 1

MIDDLE LANES
New Testament Readings

INSIDE TRACK
Favorite Readings Old & New Testaments

NOTES

Old Testament Readings (FAST TRACK)

SUNDAY
- [ ] Daniel 11
- [ ] Daniel 12
- [ ]
- [ ]
- [ ]

MONDAY
- [ ] Hosea 1
- [ ] Hosea 2
- [ ] Hosea 3
- [ ] Hosea 4
- [ ] Hosea 5

TUESDAY
- [ ] Hosea 6
- [ ] Hosea 7
- [ ] Hosea 8
- [ ] Hosea 9
- [ ] Hosea 10

WEDNESDAY
- [ ] Hosea 11
- [ ] Hosea 12
- [ ] Hosea 13
- [ ] Hosea 14
- [ ]

THURSDAY
- [ ] Joel 1
- [ ] Joel 2
- [ ] Joel 3
- [ ]
- [ ]

FRIDAY
- [ ] Amos 1
- [ ] Amos 2
- [ ] Amos 3
- [ ] Amos 4
- [ ] Amos 5

SATURDAY
- [ ] Amos 6
- [ ] Amos 7
- [ ] Amos 8
- [ ] Amos 9
- [ ]

New Testament Readings (MIDDLE LANES)

MONDAY
- [ ] 2 Peter 3
- [ ] 1 John 1

TUESDAY
- [ ] 1 John 2
- [ ] 1 John 3

WEDNESDAY
- [ ] 1 John 4
- [ ] 1 John 5

THURSDAY
- [ ] 2 John 1
- [ ] 3 John 1

FRIDAY
- [ ] Jude 1
- [ ] Revelation 1

Favorite Readings (INSIDE TRACK)

MONDAY
- [ ] Daniel 2:44
- [ ] 1 John 1:6-7

TUESDAY
- [ ] Hosea 4:6
- [ ] 1 John 2:15-16

WEDNESDAY
- [ ] Hosea 4:12
- [ ] 1 John 5:11-13

THURSDAY
- [ ] Joel 2:28
- [ ] 3 John 1:4

FRIDAY
- [ ] Amos 3:3
- [ ] Revelation 1:7

Don't Just Read the Bible Through...

The Bible is our prayer book, so read through it and lay hold of the promises of God! Make it a discipline to read the Bible, then go back and pray through what you have just read. And whenever you pray, try to tie promises of God to your prayer.

So, if you think of Psalm 127: "Children are like arrows in the hand of a warrior." Then pray, *"God, you gave me these kids for the purpose of bringing them up to love and serve you. You said they were to be like arrows in your army of blessing and salvation. God, give me the ability to do with our kids what you said you gave them to us for!"*

Or when you pray for the church, think of Deuteronomy 33:16: "Blessed be Joseph with the favor of him who dwells in the burning bush." And I pray, *"We have experienced real blessing as a church, but what if it runs out? God, it is possible, like Joseph, to dwell in your favor all of our lives? So, I am asking that we, as a church, dwell in that favor all of our days, too, so that the favor of the one who dwelt in the burning bush would be with us like it was with Joseph."*

Don't *just* read through the Bible. **Pray** *through it!* That's what followers of the **C3 Ministries** do! Go to <*www.C3Ministries.org.* >and join hundreds of others who are praying their way through the Bible. . . as they read through the Bible.

1ST BIBLE READING MARATHON - The Bible: From Darkness to The

FAST TRACK
Old Testament Readings

OBADIAH 1-ZEPHANIAH 3 # WEEK 25   **REVELATION 2-11**

MIDDLE LANES
New Testament Readings

INSIDE TRACK
Favorite Readings
Old & New Testaments

NOTES

SUNDAY
- ☐ Obadiah 1
- ☐
- ☐
- ☐
- ☐

MONDAY
- ☐ Jonah 1
- ☐ Jonah 2
- ☐ Jonah 3
- ☐ Jonah 4
- ☐

TUESDAY
- ☐ Micah 1
- ☐ Micah 2
- ☐ Micah 3
- ☐ Micah 4
- ☐ Micah 5

WEDNESDAY
- ☐ Micah 6
- ☐ Micah 7
- ☐
- ☐
- ☐

THURSDAY
- ☐ Nahum 1
- ☐ Nahum 2
- ☐ Nahum 3
- ☐
- ☐

FRIDAY
- ☐ Habakkuk 1
- ☐ Habakkuk 2
- ☐ Habakkuk 3
- ☐
- ☐

SATURDAY
- ☐ Zephaniah 1
- ☐ Zephaniah 2
- ☐ Zephaniah 3
- ☐
- ☐

MIDDLE LANES

MONDAY
- ☐ Revelation 2
- ☐ Revelation 3

TUESDAY
- ☐ Revelation 4
- ☐ Revelation 5

WEDNESDAY
- ☐ Revelation 6
- ☐ Revelation 7

THURSDAY
- ☐ Revelation 8
- ☐ Revelation 9

FRIDAY
- ☐ Revelation 10
- ☐ Revelation 11

INSIDE TRACK

MONDAY
- ☐ Jonah 1:17
- ☐ Revelation 2:10

TUESDAY
- ☐ Jonah 4:2
- ☐ Revelation 3:20

WEDNESDAY
- ☐ Micah 6:8
- ☐ Revelation 5:11-12

THURSDAY
- ☐ Nahum 1:3
- ☐ Revelation 7:15

FRIDAY
- ☐ Habakkuk 2:20
- ☐ Revelation 11:16-18

With our whole heart, let us join the author of Psalm 119 in extolling the Word of God:

◊ Wherewithal shall a young man cleanse his way? by taking heed thereto according to thy word.

◊ With my whole heart have I sought thee: O let me not wander from thy commandments.

◊ Thy word have I hid in mine heart, that I might not sin against thee (vv. 9-11).

◊ Forever, O Lord, thy word is settled in heaven (v. 89).

◊ O how I love thy law! it is my meditation all the day (v. 97).

◊ How sweet are thy words unto my taste! yea, sweeter than honey to my mouth! (v. 103)

◊ Thy Word is a lamp unto my feet and a light unto my pathway

◊ Therefore I love thy commandments above gold; yea, above fine gold (v. 127).

◊ I opened my mouth, and panted: for I longed for thy commandments (v. 131).

◊ My lips shall utter praise, when thou hast taught me thy statutes.

◊ My tongue shall speak of thy word: for all thy commandments are righteousness (vv. 171-72).

Growing Panes

FAST TRACK

Old Testament Readings

MIDDLE LANES **INSIDE TRACK** **NOTES**

New Testament Readings

Favorite Readings Old & New Testaments

SUNDAY
- [ ] Haggai 1
- [ ] Haggai 2
- [ ]
- [ ]
- [ ]

MONDAY
- [ ] Zechariah 1
- [ ] Zechariah 2
- [ ] Zechariah 3
- [ ] Zechariah 4
- [ ] Zechariah 5

TUESDAY
- [ ] Zechariah 6
- [ ] Zechariah 7
- [ ] Zechariah 8
- [ ] Zechariah 9
- [ ] Zechariah 10

WEDNESDAY
- [ ] Zechariah 11
- [ ] Zechariah 12
- [ ] Zechariah 13
- [ ] Zechariah 14
- [ ]

THURSDAY
- [ ] Malachi 1
- [ ] Malachi 2
- [ ] Malachi 3
- [ ] Malachi 4
- [ ]

FRIDAY
- [ ]
- [ ]
- [ ]
- [ ]
- [ ]

SATURDAY
- [ ]
- [ ]
- [ ]
- [ ]
- [ ]

MIDDLE LANES

MONDAY
- [ ] Revelation 12
- [ ] Revelation 13

TUESDAY
- [ ] Revelation 14
- [ ] Revelation 15

WEDNESDAY
- [ ] Revelation 16
- [ ] Revelation 17

THURSDAY
- [ ] Revelation 18
- [ ] Revelation 19

FRIDAY
- [ ] Revelation 20
- [ ] Revelation 21
- [ ] Revelation 22

INSIDE TRACK

MONDAY
- [ ] Zechariah 9:9
- [ ] Revelation 12:7-9

TUESDAY
- [ ] Zechariah 12:10
- [ ] Revelation 14:1-3

WEDNESDAY
- [ ] Malachi 3:10
- [ ] Revelation 14:13

THURSDAY
- [ ] Malachi 3:8
- [ ] Revelation 20:1-3

FRIDAY
- [ ] Malachi 2:16
- [ ] Revelation 22:6-7

The grass withereth, the flower fadeth: but the Word of our God shall stand for ever. *(Isaiah 40:8)*

The Greatest Fact of the Bible...*God Sent His Son!*

In the beginning was the Word, and the Word was with God, and the Word was God. He was in the beginning with God. All things were made through him, and without him was not any thing made that was made. In him was life, and the life was the light of men. The light shines in the darkness, and the darkness has not overcome it . . . And the Word became flesh and dwelt among us, and we have seen his glory, glory as of the only Son from the Father, full of grace and truth. **(John 1:1-4; 14)**

FINAL QUIZ: *One Question taken each from the Old Testament Readings and One from the New Testament*

1. **How many people were saved in the ark Noah built?**
   A) seven B) eight C) ten
2. **Which of Jacob's sons did not go to Egypt to get grain?**
   A) Benjamin B) Reuben C) Judah
3. **What did they build while Moses was on the Mount?**
   A) tower to heaven B) brass serpent C) golden calf
4. **What goes with the deaths of Nadab and Abihu?**
   A) double-edged swords B) water C) strange fire
5. **What mountain did God give the Ten Commandments?**
   A) Moriah B) Horeb C) Zion
6. **Where Moses was shown the promise land?**
   A) Nebo B) Moriah C) Pisgah
7. **King Saul descended from what tribe of Israel?**
   A) Rueben B) Benjamin C) Judah
8. **King David committed adultery with...?**
   A) Rahab B) Bathsheba C) Deborah
9. **What prophet was taken up in a whirlwind?**
   A) Jeremiah B) Elijah C) Elisha
10. **How did King Saul die?**
    A) By the Philistines B) By his armor-bearer C) By himself
11. **The first temple was built under what King?**
    A) Saul B) David C) Solomon
12. **Esther pleaded for her Jewish brethren to what king?**
    A) King Ahab B) King Xerxes C) King Nebuchadnezzar
13. **Which of these was not one of Job's three "friends?"**
    A) Eliphaz B) Bildad C) Zophar
14. **What is the "good Shepherd" Psalm?**
    A) Psalm 1 B) Psalm 23 C) Psalm 139
15. **What does it say God does about evil In Psalm 37:13?**
    A) Is angry B) Takes vengeance C) laughs
16. **How would you classify Psalm 100?**
    A) Praise B) Thanksgiving C) Worship
17. **What does Psalm 139 describe?**
    A) God's power B) God's all-seeing eye C) God's wrath
18. **What does a "harsh answer" do in Proverbs 15?**
    A) Rejects discipline B) Crushes the spirit C) Stirs up anger
19. **What is the "whole duty of man" in Ecclesiastes 12?**
    A) Be good neighbor B) Be moral C) Keep commandments
20. **NOT a concern by Isaiah (6) in the presence of God?**
    A) His uncleanness B) God's greatness C) Hot coal
21. **What will endure forever (Isaiah 40)?**
    A) Grass of fields B) People C) Word of God
22. **What did Ezekiel *eat* when he was called by God?**
    A) Honey B) A scroll C) Sacred meat
23. **Why was Daniel cast into the lion's den?**
    A) For Treason B) Because he prayed C) Jealousy
24. **Who was the wife of Hosea?**
    A) Jezebel B) Gomer C) Ruth
25. **To what city did God tell Jonah to go?**
    A) Tarshish B) Nineveh C) Antioch
26. **Who led in rebuilding the Temple according to Haggai?**
    A) Zechariah B) Zerubbabel C) Zephaniah

1. **In what city did Jesus grow up?**
   A) Bethlehem B) Judea C) Nazareth
2. **Which disciple identified Christ as the "son of God"?**
   A) Peter B) James C) John
3. **What feast was being observed when Jesus died?**
   A) Pentecost B) Passover C) Tabernacles
4. **What woman caused the death of John the Baptist?**
   A) Martha B) Herodias C) Salome
5. **How did Judah signal his betrayal of Jesus?**
   A) Pointed Him out B) Described Him C) Kissed Him
6. **What was Zacchaeus's occupation?**
   A) tax collector B) shepherd C) Levite Priest
7. **How many men (angels) did women see at Jesus' tomb?**
   A) one B) two C) three
8. **What was Nicodemus told to do?**
   A) Give to poor B) Take up his cross C) Be born again
9. **Where was Lazarus after he died?**
   A) In Torment B) In Paradise C) In Purgatory
10. **On what day did Peter preach first Gospel sermon?**
    A) Passover B) Pentecost C) Day of Atonement
11. **What church sent out the first missionary journey?**
    A) Jerusalem B) Antioch C) Ephesus
12. **What is the power of God for salvation?**
    A) The Miracles B) Witnessing Saints C) The Gospel
13. **How did the promises to Abraham come about?**
    A) By faith B) By the Law of Moses C) By his works
14. **The Corinthian church reacted to sexual immorality...?**
    A) being proud B) getting angry C) judging others
15. **What kind of body we will NOT have in resurrection?**
    A) natural body B) Spiritual body C) God designed body
16. **What does Paul call our bodies in 2 Corinthians 5?**
    A) a jar of clay B) earthly tent C) flesh and bones
17. **Who did Paul oppose to his face in Galatians 1?**
    A) Barnabas B) Apollos C) Peter
18. **How are husbands NOT to love their wives?**
    A) As Christ loved B) As a servant C) As their own bodies
19. **What topic should we use to encourage one another?**
    A) Death of Christ B) Love of God C) Return of Christ
20. **How does a man resist being despised for his youth?**
    A) Speak up B) Set and example C) Get married
21. **What is left out in Paul's words on his "departure"?**
    A) Fought good fight B) Finished the race C)_____
22. **What faith is NOT according to Hebrews 11?**
    A) Feelings B) Hope C) Seeing the unseen
23. **Elders shepherd according to two of these (1 Peter 5)?**
    A) Its God's Will B) Lording C) As Examples
24. **How do we keep from believing false spirits?**
    A) Test them B) Resist them C) Experience them
25. **Which church in Revelation had "lost their first love?"**
    A) Ephesus B) Sardis C) Smyrna
26. **What does NOT describe the Words of this Book? (22)**
    A) Faithful B) True C) Partial Revelation